NATIONAL GEOGRAPHIC
SCIENCE

ASS

School Publishing

PROGRAM AUTHORS

Randy Bell, Ph.D.
Malcolm B. Butler, Ph.D.
Kathy Cabe Trundle, Ph.D.
Judith S. Lederman, Ph.D.
David W. Moore, Ph.D.

Acknowledgments
Grateful acknowledgment is given to the authors, artists, photographers, museums, publishers, and agents for permission to reprint copyrighted material. Every effort has been made to secure the appropriate permission. If any omissions have been made or if corrections are required, please contact the Publisher.

Photographic Credits
Front, Back Cover Carsten Peter/National Geographic Image Collection; **T1** Kevin M. Law/Alamy Images; **8** (l) PhotoDisc/Getty Images, (cl) G.K. & Vikki Hart/Photodisc/Getty Images, (cr) Tommounsey/iStockphoto, (r) Joshua Haviv/Shutterstock; **20** (l) Rick & Nora Bowers/Alamy Images, (r) R B Forbes/ASM Mammal Image Library; **23** (t) Arpad Benedek/iStockphoto, (cl) Sally Scott/Shutterstock, (cr) John Foxx Images/Imagestate, (bl) PhotoDisc/Getty Images, (br) Jupiterimages; **24** (t) Suzi McGregor/iStockphoto, (cl) Ingram Publishing/Superstock, (cr) PhotoDisc/Getty Images, (bl) cornishman/iStockphoto, (br) Four Oaks/Shutterstock; **25** (l) Digital Vision/Getty Images, (r) mashe/Shutterstock; **33** PhotoDisc/Getty Images; **41** Jemini Joseph/iStockphoto; **51** (tl) Kristian Sekulic/Shutterstock, (tr) David Woods/Shutterstock, (bl) PhotoDisc/Getty Images, (br) Midhat Becar/iStockphoto; **55** (l) Natural Selection Steven Raniszewski/Design Pics Inc./Alamy Images, (r) Doug Sokell/Visuals Unlimited; **78** Lars Christensen/Shutterstock; **79** Creatas/Jupiterimages; **85** (l) Biophoto Associates/Photo Researchers, Inc., (r) Doug Sokell/Visuals Unlimited; **101** Group 1 (tl) FoodCollection/StockFood America, (tr) Pedro Tavares/Shutterstock, (cl) Ingram Publishing/Superstock, (cr) DNY59/iStockphoto, (bl) Luca di Filippo/iStockphoto, (br) Ichiro Ichiro/White/Photolibrary, Group 2 (tl) Luca di Filippo/iStockphoto, (tr) FoodCollection/StockFood America, (cl) Ingram Publishing/Superstock, (cr) Pedro Tavares/Shutterstock, (bl) Ichiro Ichiro/White/Photolibrary, (br) DNY59/iStockphoto; **118** (l) Stockbyte/Getty Images, (c, r) Artville.

Art Credits
4 Dartmouth Publishing, Inc.; **14** Dartmouth Publishing, Inc.; **15** Dartmouth Publishing, Inc.; **16** Dartmouth Publishing, Inc.; **40** Dartmouth Publishing, Inc.; **81** Dartmouth Publishing, Inc.; **86** Dartmouth Publishing, Inc.; **99** Dartmouth Publishing, Inc.; **100** Dartmouth Publishing, Inc.; **106** Dartmouth Publishing, Inc.; **120** Dartmouth Publishing, Inc.; **121** Dartmouth Publishing, Inc.; **122** Dartmouth Publishing, Inc.; **131** Dartmouth Publishing, Inc.

Neither the Publisher nor the authors shall be liable for any damage that may be caused or sustained or result from conducting any of the activities in this publication without specifically following instructions, undertaking the activities without proper supervision, or failing to comply with the cautions contained herein.

Program Authors
Randy Bell, Ph.D.
Malcolm B. Butler, Ph.D.
Kathy Cabe Trundle, Ph.D.
Judith S. Lederman, Ph.D.
David W. Moore, Ph.D.

The National Geographic Society
John M. Fahey, Jr., President & Chief Executive Officer
Gilbert M. Grosvenor, Chairman of the Board

Copyright © 2011 The Hampton-Brown Company, Inc., a wholly owned subsidiary of the National Geographic Society, publishing under the imprints National Geographic School Publishing and Hampton-Brown.

Teachers are authorized to reproduce the assessment materials in this Handbook in limited quantities and solely for use in their own classrooms.

Other than as authorized above, no part of this book may be reproduced or transmitted in any form or by any means, electronic or mechanical, including photocopying, recording, or by an information storage and retrieval system, without permission in writing from the Publisher. National Geographic and the Yellow Border are registered trademarks of the National Geographic Society.

National Geographic School Publishing
Hampton-Brown
www.NGSP.com

Printed in the USA.

ISBN 978-0-7362-7789-1

11 12 13 14 15 16 17
10 9 8 7 6 5 4 3 2

HPS232385

Contents

Introduction to National Geographic Science Grade 4 Assessment T1
- Program Goals T1
- Assessment Design T1
- Assessment Tools T2
- Chapter and Benchmark Tests T3
- Scoring Tests and Reporting Results T3

Life Science Chapter Tests and Self-Assessments 1
- Chapter 1: How Do Plants Grow and Reproduce? 3
- Chapter 2: How Do Animals Grow and Change? 7
- Chapter 3: How Do Living Things Depend on Their Environment? 11
- Chapter 4: How Do Adaptations Help Living Things Survive? 18
- Chapter 5: How Do Living Things Interact with Their Environment? 26
- Chapter 6: How Do the Parts of an Organism Work Together? 31

Life Science Benchmark Test 37
- Life Science Benchmark Test 38

Earth Science Chapter Tests and Self-Assessments 45
- Chapter 1: How Do Earth and Its Moon Move? 47
- Chapter 2: How Are Rocks Alike and Different? 53
- Chapter 3: What Are Renewable and Nonrenewable Resources? 59
- Chapter 4: How Do Slow Processes Change Earth's Surface? 66
- Chapter 5: What Changes Do Volcanoes and Earthquakes Cause? 71
- Chapter 6: What Can We Observe About Weather? 76

Earth Science Benchmark Test 83
- Earth Science Benchmark Test 84

Physical Science Chapter Tests and Self-Assessments 93
- Chapter 1: How Can You Describe and Measure Properties of Matter? 95
- Chapter 2: What Are Physical and Chemical Changes? 102
- Chapter 3: How Do Forces Act? 105
- Chapter 4: What Is Magnetism? 109
- Chapter 5: What Are Some Forms of Energy? 112
- Chapter 6: What Is Sound? 116
- Chapter 7: What Is Electricity? 119

Physical Science Benchmark Test 123
- Physical Science Benchmark Test 124

Contents

Scoring and Reporting Tools 133
Life Science Student Profiles and Answer Keys: Chapter Tests 1–6. 134
Life Science Student Profile and Answer Key: Benchmark Test 146
Life Science Class Profile 148
Earth Science Student Profiles and Answer Keys: Chapter Tests 1–6 149
Earth Science Student Profile and Answer Key: Benchmark Test. 161
Earth Science Class Profile 163
Physical Science Student Profiles and Answer Keys: Chapter Tests 1–7 164
Physical Science Student Profile and Answer Key: Benchmark Test 178
Physical Science Class Profile 180

Inquiry Rubrics and Self-Reflections. 181
Life Science Inquiry Rubrics 182
Life Science Inquiry Self-Reflections. 189
Earth Science Inquiry Rubrics 202
Earth Science Inquiry Self-Reflections. 209
Physical Science Inquiry Rubrics 222
Physical Science Inquiry Self-Reflections 230

Introduction

Program Goals

National Geographic Science offers research-based instruction to build scientific and content literacy for all students. The program is carefully designed to target specific state science standards while enabling students to explore the nature of science and inquiry.

Assessment Design

National Geographic Science assessments have been designed so that frequent, varied assessment informs instruction every step of the way. Chapter and Benchmark Tests provide a window into student thinking about scientific concepts throughout the instructional cycle.

Instruct

Develop an understanding of and provide explicit and systematic instruction in:
- The Big Ideas in Science
- Science Academic Vocabulary
- Scientific Inquiry

Assess to Monitor Progress

Chapter Tests provide opportunities for students to apply their understanding of key concepts. Use **Chapter Tests** for timely information about student progress as you deliver instruction.

Show Success

The **Benchmark Test** measures a student's overall progress in understanding the Life, Earth, and Physical units' Big Ideas.

Assessment Tools

National Geographic Science offers an array of assessments in a variety of formats.

ASSESSMENT TOOLS	Assessment Handbook	PDFs myNGconnect.com	ExamView®
CHAPTER TESTS • Chapter Tests provide immediate feedback on students' understanding of standards-based scientific concepts. • The tests are administered at the end of each chapter to provide an early indicator of the students' progress.	✓	✓	✓
CHAPTER SELF-ASSESSMENTS • The Chapter Self-Assessments empower students to rate their own understanding of the chapter's concepts and share their opinions about future interests.	✓	✓	
BENCHMARK TESTS • The Benchmark Tests measure students' progress toward understanding each unit's Big Ideas. • Each test is administered at the end of the unit.	✓	✓	✓
INQUIRY RUBRICS • Inquiry Rubrics assess students' performance of skills in Inquiry activities.	✓	✓	
INQUIRY SELF-REFLECTIONS • Inquiry Self-Reflections engage students in evaluating their own performance of inquiry skills and in sharing their opinions about the activity process.	✓	✓	

Chapter and Benchmark Tests

The Chapter and Benchmark assessments for National Geographic Science each provide a unique view into students' progress in understanding key science concepts. The Chapter Tests provide timely snapshots of the students' depth of understanding of the science concepts in each chapter as they progress through the unit.

The Benchmark Test consists of items that provide information about overall student progress at the end of the unit. Multiple-choice and constructed-response items focus on key concepts as they have been presented in the instructional materials. This test provides students with experience in answering items in formats commonly found on many standardized tests.

Scoring Tests and Reporting Results

Teachers can score Chapter and Benchmark Tests and report results by hand. Use the Answer Keys and rubrics in the Scoring and Reporting Tools section on pages 134–180 to score the tests. Then fill out the Student and Class Profiles to report test results. See page 133 for more information.

Through ExamView®, the multiple-choice section of the Chapter and Benchmark Tests can also be scored electronically. Students can take the Chapter and Benchmark Tests online through the ExamView® Test Player on a local area network, or they can mark answers on an ExamView® machine-scorable answer sheet, which is later scanned to enter data electronically.

Online reports in ExamView® can be generated for the Chapter and Benchmark Tests from electronically scored tests. Online reports can also be created for hand-scored results for either the Chapter and Benchmark Tests by manually entering the test scores into ExamView®.

Life Science Chapter Tests and Self-Assessments

> Chapter 1: How Do Plants Grow and Reproduce?....................3
> Chapter 2: How Do Animals Grow and Change? 7
> Chapter 3: How Do Living Things Depend on
>   Their Environment? 11
> Chapter 4: How Do Adaptations Help Living Things Survive? 18
> Chapter 5: How Do Living Things Interact with
>   Their Environment? 26
> Chapter 6: How Do the Parts of an Organism Work Together? 31

Chapter Self-Assessment

Purpose and Description

The Chapter Self-Assessment helps students review their own progress toward meeting specific learning objectives in the chapter. Students also indicate an area of interest for further study. Make a copy of the Chapter Self-Assessment for each student and have them fill it out before taking the Chapter Test.

Chapter Tests

Purpose and Description

A Chapter Test is available for each of the six chapters in the Life Science Unit. Each Chapter Test is designed to check student progress on the specific instruction within the chapter and to provide an early indicator that additional instruction may be necessary. Chapter Tests generally use multiple-choice and short constructed-response items to measure student understanding of the Life Science concepts taught in this unit.

Administering the Tests

Administer the test for each chapter after instruction. Allow 10 to 20 minutes for administration, depending on the length of the test. Make a copy of the test for each student.

All directions may be read to the students. All test items, including any charts and diagrams, may be read to students if deemed necessary. Use a copy of the test to point out directions, test items, and response areas.

Introduce the test by telling students the purpose of the test.

- To begin the test, read the directions.
- Tell students how they are expected to respond to that type of item, for example, by filling in a circle.

Life Science Chapter Tests and Self-Assessments

- Give students time to work individually on the test, and allow a reasonable amount of time for them to complete it.
- Look to see that students are responding to the items in the correct manner.
- Read the directions and items in the test as necessary, explaining to students how they are expected to respond to any new item formats.

Students may not use their books during the test.

Scoring the Tests and Using the Results

Score the Chapter Tests with the Answer Keys in the Scoring and Reporting Tools section, beginning on page 134. Use the Student Profiles in the same section to determine if students need additional instruction in any of the science concepts presented. For more information on scoring, see page 133.

Name _____ Date _____ **Chapter 1**

Chapter Self-Assessment — How Do Plants Grow and Reproduce?

Directions: Write a ✓ in the box to show the answer that is true for you.

	Yes	Not Yet
❶ I can identify the major parts of a seed plant and understand what they do.		
❷ I can classify plants according to their characteristics.		
❸ I can compare the life cycles of flowering plants and conifers.		
❹ I can identify individual differences in plants of the same kind.		
❺ I can explain that some characteristics of plants can be affected by the environment.		
❻ I can compare the parts that flowering plants and conifers use to reproduce.		
❼ I can describe how flowering plants are pollinated and fertilized.		
❽ I can describe how flowering plants form seeds and fruit.		
❾ I can describe how flowering plant seeds are spread.		
❿ I can describe how flowering plants germinate and grow.		

Directions: Think about the things you have studied in this chapter. Then finish the sentence.

⓫ I am interested in learning more about _____

_____

_____

_____

Name _____ Date _____ Chapter 1

Chapter Test How Do Plants Grow and Reproduce?

Directions: Read each question. Then choose the correct answer.

1 Emily is studying the reproduction of a pear tree. She cuts open a pear from the tree to observe its seeds. Which is **most likely** the method of seed dispersal used by a pear tree?

Ⓐ wind blowing the seeds to new places

Ⓑ water carrying the seeds to new places

Ⓒ hooked seeds catching in animals' coats and then falling in new places

Ⓓ animals eating the plant's fruit and dropping the seeds in new places

2 Which of these is a part of a flowering plant where seeds are formed?

Ⓐ fruit

Ⓑ cone

Ⓒ root

Ⓓ leaf

3 Karen is classifying different plants. She places the four plants listed below in two groups.

Group A	Group B
fern	orange tree
moss	pine tree

Karen places a third plant in Group A. Which characteristic does this third plant **most likely** have?

Ⓐ fruits

Ⓑ cones

Ⓒ spores

Ⓓ seeds

GO ON

4

Grade 4 Life Science

Name _____ Date _____ **Chapter 1**

Chapter Test: How Do Plants Grow and Reproduce?

4 A butterfly flies from one flower to another to drink nectar. How does this help the flowers?

Ⓐ The butterfly protects the seeds.
Ⓑ The butterfly pollinates the flowers.
Ⓒ The butterfly carries away the seeds.
Ⓓ The butterfly makes food for the flowers.

5 Anna and Matthew are looking at two plants outside their house. One is a flowering plant, and the other is a conifer. Which statement is true about the two plants?

Ⓐ Both plants produce fruit.
Ⓑ Both plants have the same life cycle.
Ⓒ Flowering plant seeds germinate and conifer seeds do not.
Ⓓ The flowering plant and the conifer are pollinated in different ways.

6 Barbara saw two of the same type of apple tree at the park. Although they were the same type of tree, there were some differences. Which characteristic could **most likely** be different?

Ⓐ the type of flowers
Ⓑ the size of their leaves
Ⓒ the way they reproduce
Ⓓ the location of the seeds

7 How does a fruit develop in a plant?

Ⓐ The fruit grows inside the female cones.
Ⓑ The fruit is pollinated by seeds after fertilization.
Ⓒ The fruit begins to grow before germination of the plant.
Ⓓ The fruit begins to form on the wall of the ovaries that surround the seeds.

8 Which of these is used in the reproduction of both flowering plants and conifers?

Ⓐ pollen
Ⓑ petal
Ⓒ cone
Ⓓ fruit

9 Tina plants corn seeds in the soil and waters them well. She knows that the corn will use photosynthesis to make food as it grows. Which process must happen to the seeds she planted before photosynthesis can occur?

Ⓐ Flowers bloom.
Ⓑ Cones develop.
Ⓒ Seeds germinate.
Ⓓ Flowers are pollinated.

GO ON

Grade 4 Life Science

Name _____ Date _____ **Chapter 1**

| **Chapter Test** | **How Do Plants Grow and Reproduce?** |

10 Carlos is studying the characteristics of tulips. He is classifying the characteristics into two groups: those that are inherited and those that are affected by the environment.

Which of these characteristics would **most likely** be affected by the environment?

Ⓐ the way they smell

Ⓑ the size of their leaves

Ⓒ the way they reproduce

Ⓓ the color of their flowers

Directions: Read the question. Then write your answer on the lines.

11 Denise grows an apple tree in a pot indoors. The tree looks healthy, and it blossoms, but the blossoms never turn into apples.

What **two** processes must occur in order for the blossoms to turn into apples?

1) _____

2) _____

Why did these processes not occur in this apple tree?

_____

_____

Test Score

_____ /12

6

Grade 4 Life Science

Name _____ Date _____ **Chapter 2**

Chapter Self-Assessment — **How Do Animals Grow and Change?**

Directions: Write a ✓ in the box to show the answer that is true for you.

	Yes	Not Yet
❶ I can describe the different life cycles of animals.		
❷ I can identify the different stages of animals' life cycles.		
❸ I know that living things grow and change, and they need water, nutrients, and air to survive.		
❹ I can compare similarities and differences in offspring of different animal life cycles.		
❺ I can describe how an insect molts as part of incomplete metamorphosis.		
❻ I know that animals get some traits from their parents and that they also have individual traits.		
❼ I can describe inherited animal behaviors.		
❽ I know that the environment can cause animals to acquire traits.		
❾ I can describe behaviors that animals learn.		

Directions: Think about the things you have studied in this chapter. Then finish the sentence.

❿ I am interested in learning more about _____

_____

_____

_____

Grade 4 Assessment

Name _____ Date _____ Chapter 2

Chapter Test: How Do Animals Grow and Change?

Directions: Read each question. Then choose the correct answer.

1 A luna moth goes through complete metamorphosis during its life cycle. A praying mantis goes through incomplete metamorphosis. What is one way the two insects' life cycles are the same?

Ⓐ Both have a larva stage.

Ⓑ Both have a pupa stage.

Ⓒ Both have a nymph stage.

Ⓓ Both have an adult stage.

2 A dolphin pushes its calf to the surface of the water right after the calf is born. Why does the mother **most likely** do this?

Ⓐ so the calf can hear better

Ⓑ so the calf can leave its mother

Ⓒ so the calf can get air to breathe

Ⓓ so the calf can look for other dolphins

3 Look at the pictures of a kitten, an adult cat, a frog larva and an adult frog. Which statement **best** compares the life cycles of a cat and frog?

  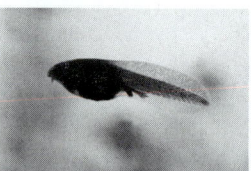 

Kitten　　　　Adult cat　　　　Frog larva　　　　Adult frog

Ⓐ Frogs go through metamorphosis, but cats do not.

Ⓑ Cats and frogs go through metamorphosis since they both have tails.

Ⓒ A kitten is in the nymph stage of metamorphosis, and frogs go directly to the adult stage.

Ⓓ A cat goes through complete metamorphosis, and a frog goes through incomplete metamorphosis.

GO ON

Grade 4 Life Science

Chapter Test — How Do Animals Grow and Change?

4 Cicadas go through incomplete metamorphosis. To pass from the nymph stage to the adult stage, what must a cicada nymph do?

Ⓐ lay eggs

Ⓑ build a cocoon

Ⓒ become a pupa

Ⓓ shed its outer covering

5 Sarah observes a group of the same type of dogs. Which inherited trait would **most likely** be different in the group of dogs?

Ⓐ the color of fur

Ⓑ the ability to bark

Ⓒ the number of their legs

Ⓓ the sharpness of their teeth

6 An adult spider builds a web. The spider dies before its eggs are hatched. Which statement **best** explains why the spider's offspring can build webs?

Ⓐ They learn to build webs by watching other spiders.

Ⓑ They get the web-building trait from the environment.

Ⓒ They match the kind of web to the insects they want to eat.

Ⓓ They inherited the ability to build a web.

Name _____ Date _____

Chapter 2

Chapter Test — How Do Animals Grow and Change?

7 Which statement is an example of an acquired trait?

Ⓐ A moth larva enters a pupa stage.

Ⓑ A robin reproduces by laying blue eggs.

Ⓒ A nymph praying mantis looks like an adult praying mantis.

Ⓓ A zebra has a crack in one hoof from walking on hard rocks.

Directions: Read the question. Then write your answer on the lines.

8 A scientist places a laboratory rat in a maze. When the rat completes the maze, it is rewarded with food. After a few tries, the rat quickly finds the end of the maze and the food. Is this an inherited behavior or a learned behavior? Explain.

_____

_____

Would a rat that had grown up in the wild be able to complete the maze on the first try? Explain.

_____

_____

Test Score ____/9

10

Grade 4 Life Science

Name _____ Date _____ **Chapter 3**

Chapter Self-Assessment
How Do Living Things Depend on Their Environment?

Directions: Write a ✓ in the box to show the answer that is true for you.

	Yes	Not Yet
❶ I know that communities are groups of living things that depend on each other for food.		
❷ I know that green plants are producers because they make food.		
❸ I can describe and name examples of herbivores, carnivores, and omnivores.		
❹ I can describe the role of decomposers in a community.		
❺ I can describe how energy passes from one living thing to another in a community.		
❻ I know that several food chains form a food web.		
❼ I know the role of each organism in a food web.		
❽ I can describe examples of how plants and animals interact with each other.		
❾ I can classify living things as predators or prey and describe how they depend on each other.		
❿ I can give examples of parasites and their hosts and explain how parasites get their food.		
⓫ I can explain that individuals within a species may compete with each other for resources.		

Directions: Think about the things you have studied in this chapter. Then finish the sentence.

⓬ I am interested in learning more about _____

_____

_____

Name _____   Date _____   **Chapter 3**

Chapter Test **How Do Living Things Depend on Their Environment?**

Directions: Read each question. Then choose the correct answer.

1 What do air, water, space, and energy have in common?
  Ⓐ All are necessary for life.
  Ⓑ All are produced by plants.
  Ⓒ All are absorbed by decomposers.
  Ⓓ All are used by predators to catch prey.

2 Which of these **best** describes what makes up a community?
  Ⓐ all of the producers in an area
  Ⓑ all of the predators in an area
  Ⓒ all of the living things that depend on each other for food in an area
  Ⓓ all of the members of the same species that compete for resources in an area

3 Which living thing is a producer?
  Ⓐ a fox, because it eats both plants and animals
  Ⓑ the sun, because it produces energy all living things need
  Ⓒ a sunflower, because it uses sunlight, water, and air to make food
  Ⓓ a mushroom, because it breaks down the remains of plants and animals

GO ON

Chapter Test: How Do Living Things Depend on Their Environment?

Chapter 3

4 How are herbivores different from carnivores?

Ⓐ Herbivores eat only animals, and carnivores eat only plants.

Ⓑ Herbivores eat only plants, and carnivores eat only animals.

Ⓒ Herbivores eat only plants, and carnivores eat both plants and animals.

Ⓓ Herbivores eat both plants and animals, and carnivores eat only animals.

5 Which consumer is an herbivore?

Ⓐ goat

Ⓑ bear

Ⓒ hawk

Ⓓ leopard

6 A scientist is studying an animal that has both sharp teeth and flat teeth. What type of consumer is she **most likely** studying?

Ⓐ herbivore

Ⓑ carnivore

Ⓒ omnivore

Ⓓ decomposer

7 Tom is making a poster about consumers. Which consumer should he label as an omnivore?

Ⓐ cow

Ⓑ lion

Ⓒ snake

Ⓓ human

8 Why are decomposers important in a community?

Ⓐ They eat predators that prey on other animals.

Ⓑ They recycle nutrients by breaking down dead organisms.

Ⓒ They make energy for all of the producers and consumers.

Ⓓ They are a main food source for producers and consumers.

9 A mistletoe plant grows on the trunk of another plant. It takes water and nutrients away from the plant. Which of these **best** describes the role of the mistletoe in this relationship?

Ⓐ parasite

Ⓑ predator

Ⓒ herbivore

Ⓓ carnivore

GO ON

Grade 4 Life Science

Chapter Test: How Do Living Things Depend on Their Environment?

Chapter 3

10 A scientist is studying a pond community.

Which is the **most likely** path of energy in this community?

Ⓐ plants to insect to frog to sun

Ⓑ frog to plants to insect to sun

Ⓒ sun to insect to plants to frog

Ⓓ sun to plants to insect to frog

11 Which statement **best** describes a food web?

Ⓐ all the food an animal eats

Ⓑ all the food chains in a community

Ⓒ all the producers in a community

Ⓓ all the food that gets recycled

12 Which relationship **best** shows an example of a parasite and its host?

Ⓐ a flea biting a cat

Ⓑ a deer tasting berries

Ⓒ a bird catching a worm

Ⓓ a dog fed by its owner

13 Which of these describes a relationship in which both living things benefit?

Ⓐ A deer eats the leaves of a cedar tree.

Ⓑ A person touches poison ivy and then gets a rash.

Ⓒ A bird makes a nest in a tree.

Ⓓ A bee drinks nectar from a flower and carries pollen to other flowers.

14 Jenny is making a list of the resources that animals in a prairie community compete for. Which of these would she **most likely** put on her list?

Ⓐ air

Ⓑ water

Ⓒ sunlight

Ⓓ shelter

GO ON

Grade 4 Life Science

Name _____ Date _____

Chapter 3

Chapter Test — How Do Living Things Depend on Their Environment?

15 Which statement describes a predator and its prey in this food web?

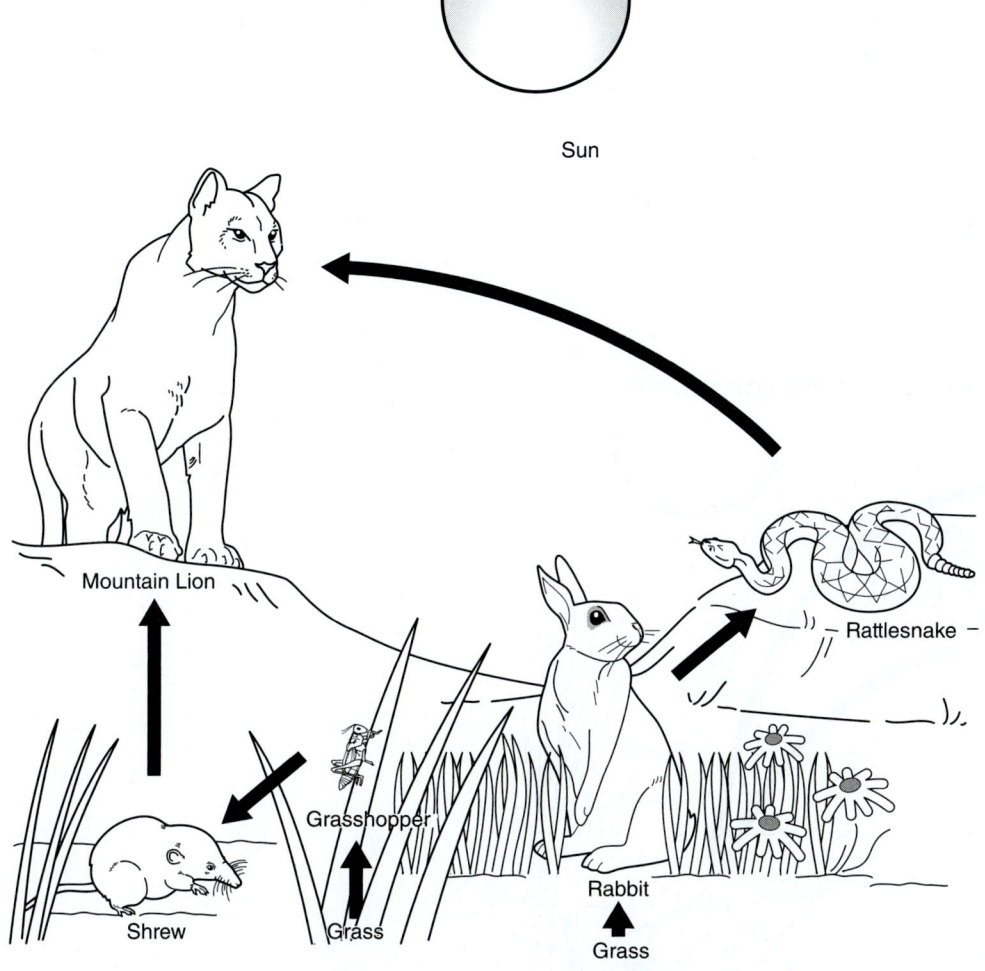

Ⓐ The shrew is a predator, and the rattlesnake is its prey.

Ⓑ The rabbit is a predator, and the grasshopper is its prey.

Ⓒ The grasshopper is a predator, and the shrew is its prey.

Ⓓ The mountain lion is a predator, and the rattlesnake is its prey.

GO ON

Grade 4 Life Science

Name _____ Date _____ **Chapter 3**

Chapter Test How Do Living Things Depend on Their Environment?

16 Tim finds a tick on his dog. Tim knows that the tick is a parasite. What will the tick **most likely** do if it stays on the dog?

Ⓐ The tick will get food from the dog.

Ⓑ The tick will help the dog find food.

Ⓒ The tick will become food for the dog.

Ⓓ The tick will produce food for the dog.

17 Which statement is **most likely** true for this community?

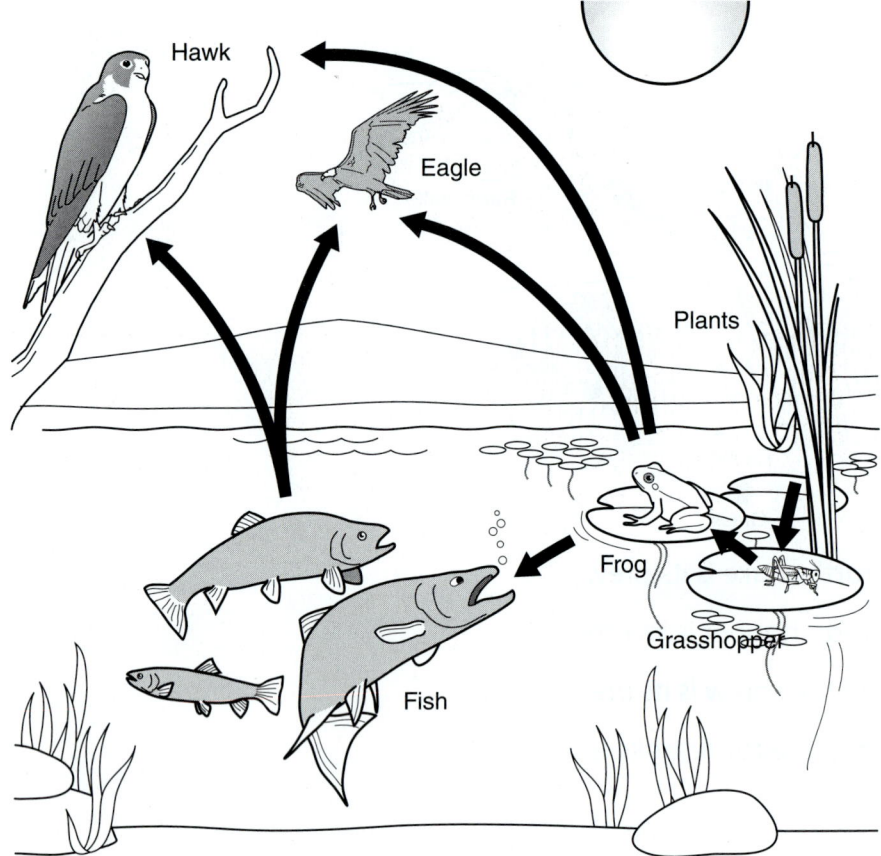

Ⓐ The fish are prey, and the frogs are their predators.

Ⓑ The plants are prey, and the fish are their predators.

Ⓒ The frogs are prey, and the hawks are their predators.

Ⓓ The eagles are prey, and the hawks are their predators.

Name _____ Date _____ Chapter 3

Chapter Test — How Do Living Things Depend on Their Environment?

18 A scientist is studying an ocean food chain.

sun → diatoms → zooplankton → mackerel → tuna → shark

What would **most likely** happen if the population of tuna decreased?

Ⓐ The number of sharks would increase.

Ⓑ The number of mackerel would increase.

Ⓒ The number of sharks would remain the same.

Ⓓ The number of mackerel would remain the same.

Directions: Read the question. Then write your answer on the lines.

19 Several maple trees have been planted close together. Write **two** ways in which these trees might compete with each other.

1) _____

2) _____

Test Score ____ /20

Name _____ Date _____ **Chapter 4**

Chapter Self-Assessment — **How Do Adaptations Help Living Things Survive?**

Directions: Write a ✓ in the box to show the answer that is true for you.

	Yes	Not Yet
1 I can explain how adaptations help a living thing survive.		
2 I know that hunger is a signal that causes an animal to hunt for food.		
3 I can explain how animals use adaptations for food, defense, and protection.		
4 I can tell the difference between an adaptation and a variation.		
5 I can give examples of adaptations that help animals grow, stay healthy, and reproduce.		
6 I can explain the advantages of animals using sound to communicate.		
7 I can explain that flowers, seeds, and fruit are adaptations for plant reproduction.		
8 I know that fossils are the remains of organisms that once lived.		
9 I can explain how scientists use fossils in the study of Earth's history.		
10 I can give examples of modern plants and animals that look like fossilized species.		

Directions: Think about the things you have studied in this chapter. Then finish the sentence.

11 I am interested in learning more about _____

_____

_____

_____

Name _____ Date _____

Chapter 4

Chapter Test: How Do Adaptations Help Living Things Survive?

Directions: Read each question. Then choose the correct answer.

1 Which of these plant adaptations reduces water loss?

Ⓐ thorns on the stem

Ⓑ brightly colored flowers

Ⓒ waxy covering on leaves

Ⓓ seeds covered with hooks

2 Berries are a type of fruit found on a blackberry plant. How do berries help the blackberry plant?

Ⓐ They make food for the plant.

Ⓑ They absorb water for the plant.

Ⓒ They protect the plant from predators.

Ⓓ They disperse seeds for the plant to new areas.

3 Alligators live in swamps. They are able to lie so still that they look like floating logs in the water. How does this adaptation help the alligator to survive?

Ⓐ It helps the alligator to swim better.

Ⓑ It helps the alligator to be able to reproduce.

Ⓒ It helps the alligator to surprise and catch its food.

Ⓓ It helps the alligator to travel to other nearby swamps.

GO ON

Grade 4 Life Science

Name _____ Date _____ Chapter 4

Chapter Test How Do Adaptations Help Living Things Survive?

4 Some turtles have a tongue that looks like a worm. How does this **most likely** help the turtle?

Ⓐ The tongue attracts prey, making it easier to catch food.

Ⓑ The tongue helps the turtle find other turtles for reproduction.

Ⓒ The tongue makes the turtle's predators think that the turtle is a worm.

Ⓓ The tongue makes the turtle look like it already ate and is not looking for food.

5 Rock pocket mice can have brown or black fur. More of the mice with brown fur survive in areas with light-colored rocks. More of the mice with black fur survive in areas with dark-colored rocks.

Which statement **best** compares adaptation and variation in pocket mice?

Ⓐ Variation is the different colors of fur, and adaptation is how the colors help the mice survive.

Ⓑ Adaptation is the different colors of fur, and variation is how the colors help the mice survive.

Ⓒ Different colors of fur are adaptations, but mice have no variations.

Ⓓ Different colors of fur are variations, but mice have no adaptations.

GO ON

20 Grade 4 Life Science

Name _____ Date _____ **Chapter 4**

Chapter Test — How Do Adaptations Help Living Things Survive?

6 Bats sleep during the day and hunt for food at night. Which adaptation would be **most** helpful to them in finding their food?

  Ⓐ small teeth

  Ⓑ dark coloring

  Ⓒ poor eyesight

  Ⓓ excellent hearing

7 Some monkeys screech and bare their teeth as a warning that they will fight back if attacked. What advantage would this **most likely** give the monkeys?

  Ⓐ It could let other monkeys know that they are hungry.

  Ⓑ It could convince predators not to come near the monkeys.

  Ⓒ It could allow mother monkeys to be able to find their babies.

  Ⓓ It could signal to the monkeys nearby that prey is in the area.

8 Which example **best** explains an adaptation that is for reproduction?

  Ⓐ Chameleons can change color.

  Ⓑ Cheetahs can run extremely fast for short distances.

  Ⓒ Emperor penguins can make sounds to attract a mate.

  Ⓓ Sloths can hang upside down from trees for long periods of time.

9 Lions will not usually hunt after they finish a big meal. Which of these will make the lions hunt for food?

  Ⓐ thirst

  Ⓑ hunger

  Ⓒ camouflage

  Ⓓ extinction

10 Some grasses do not taste good. How does this adaptation **most likely** help these grasses?

  Ⓐ It helps the grass to make food.

  Ⓑ It helps the grass to store water.

  Ⓒ It helps the grass to protect itself.

  Ⓓ It helps the grass to absorb sunlight.

11 Why are flowers important to some plants?

  Ⓐ They defend the plant from predators.

  Ⓑ They make food when the plant needs it.

  Ⓒ They store water until the next time it rains.

  Ⓓ They attract animals that pick up their pollen.

GO ON

Chapter Test — **How Do Adaptations Help Living Things Survive?**

Chapter 4

12 A dandelion seed is light enough to be carried by the wind. How does this **most** help the dandelion plant?

- Ⓐ It dries the seeds.
- Ⓑ It protects the seeds from other plants.
- Ⓒ It makes it difficult for birds to eat the seeds.
- Ⓓ It disperses the seeds so that new plants can grow.

13 The basilisk lizard is able to run on top of the water across a small pond. How does this adaptation **most likely** help the lizard to survive?

- Ⓐ It allows the lizard to grasp and eat its prey.
- Ⓑ It allows the lizard to get away from predators.
- Ⓒ It allows the lizard to blend in with its surroundings.
- Ⓓ It allows the lizard to show its parents that it is hungry.

14 In the past, both triceratops and sharks lived at the same time. Which statement **best** explains why triceratops became extinct but sharks still live today?

- Ⓐ The sharks ate the triceratops.
- Ⓑ The sharks had no defense against predators.
- Ⓒ Only animals that live on land become extinct.
- Ⓓ Sharks were able to adapt to the changing environment.

15 How can a plant fossil **best** be used by scientists?

- Ⓐ The fossil can tell scientists what animals eat the plant.
- Ⓑ The fossil can tell scientists how much animals liked the plant.
- Ⓒ The fossil can help scientists predict what kinds of plants will live in the future.
- Ⓓ The fossil can help scientists learn what the area was like when the fossil formed.

GO ON

Name _____ Date _____ Chapter 4

Chapter Test — How Do Adaptations Help Living Things Survive?

16 The picture shows a plant fossil. Which plant is **most** similar to the plant in the fossil?

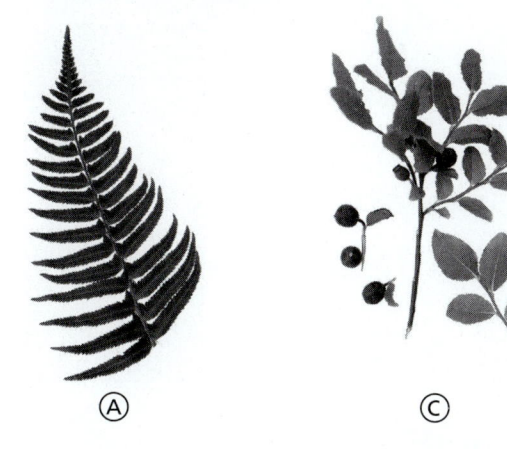

Ⓐ   Ⓒ

Ⓑ   Ⓓ

Name _____ Date _____

Chapter 4

Chapter Test — **How Do Adaptations Help Living Things Survive?**

17 The picture shows a fossilized animal. Which animal below looks **most** like the fossil in the picture?

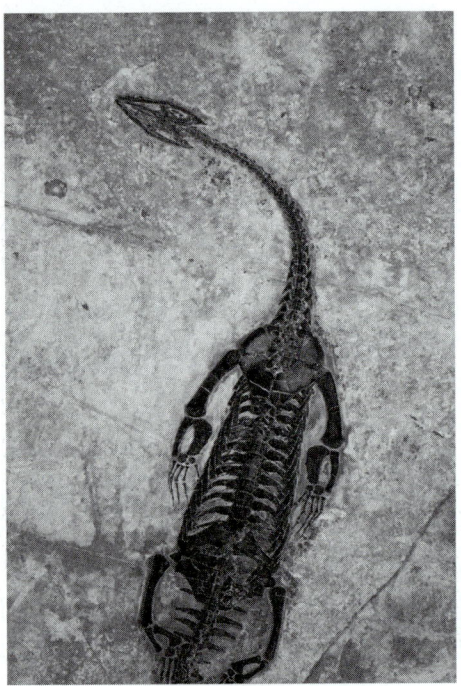

Ⓐ   Ⓒ

Ⓑ   Ⓓ

GO ON

Name _____ Date _____

Chapter 4

Chapter Test — How Do Adaptations Help Living Things Survive?

18 What are fossils?

   Ⓐ remains of living things from long ago

   Ⓑ adaptations that living things use for defense

   Ⓒ adaptations that allow living things to reproduce

   Ⓓ models of living things that scientists make in museums

Directions: Read the question. Then write your answer on the lines.

19 Look at these pictures of a chameleon using camouflage by changing colors.

Explain how this adaptation helps the chameleon protect itself in its environment.

_____

_____

Describe an example of another adaptation that an animal can use to protect itself.

_____

_____

Test Score _____ /20

25

Grade 4 Life Science

Name _____ Date _____ Chapter 5

Chapter Self-Assessment: How Do Living Things Interact with Their Environment?

Directions: Write a ✓ in the box to show the answer that is true for you.

	Yes	Not Yet
❶ I know ways that plants and animals can change the environment.		
❷ I can give examples of how plants change over the seasons.		
❸ I can give examples of how animals adapt to changing seasons.		
❹ I can describe how plants and animals can harm an environment.		
❺ I can give examples of how plants and animals can change the environment.		
❻ I know that people can change the environment in good and bad ways.		
❼ I know that people depend on their environment to meet their needs.		

Directions: Think about the things you have studied in this chapter. Then finish the sentence.

❽ I am interested in learning more about _____

_____

_____

_____

Name _____ Date _____

Chapter 5

Chapter Test — How Do Living Things Interact with Their Environment?

Directions: Read each question. Then choose the correct answer.

1 Which of these adaptations would help an animal that lives in an environment that is snowy in winter?

Ⓐ It sheds its fur.

Ⓑ It changes its color.

Ⓒ It becomes more active.

Ⓓ It moves to a colder area.

2 How does a tree **most likely** change in response to the beginning of fall?

Ⓐ Its fruit will grow.

Ⓑ Its flowers will bloom.

Ⓒ Its branches will fall off.

Ⓓ Its leaves will change color.

3 A certain kind of tree grows in a northern state and a southern state. How will the trees in the two states **most likely** change when winter comes?

Ⓐ The trees will both have flowers.

Ⓑ The leaves of both trees will turn red.

Ⓒ The northern tree will have no leaves, but the southern tree will.

Ⓓ The southern tree will have flowers and the northern tree will have fruit.

GO ON

Grade 4 Life Science

Chapter Test: How Do Living Things Interact with Their Environment?

Chapter 5

4 Grass grows on a sandy river bank. Which of these is the **main** way the grass changes the river bank?

Ⓐ It keeps the sand in place.

Ⓑ It lets the sand move and drift.

Ⓒ It breaks the sand into smaller pieces.

Ⓓ It removes useful materials from the sand.

5 How will alligators **most likely** adapt to the dry season in the southern United States?

Ⓐ They will change color.

Ⓑ They will dig holes to collect water.

Ⓒ They will sleep for long periods of time.

Ⓓ They will migrate to a different part of the country.

6 A certain plant begins to grow in an area and change the environment. Which of these changes would make the plant an invasive organism?

Ⓐ Its flowers attract more animals.

Ⓑ Its leaves provide food for insects.

Ⓒ It crowds out other plants that live there.

Ⓓ It grows quickly where other plants do not grow.

GO ON

Name _____ Date _____ **Chapter 5**

Chapter Test — How Do Living Things Interact with Their Environment?

7 Which of these causes harm to the environment?
- Ⓐ Worms dig through soil.
- Ⓑ Deer spread tree seeds.
- Ⓒ Cows eat all the grass in one place.
- Ⓓ Elephants use their trunks to find water.

8 Which animal home **most likely** has the biggest effect on its environment?
- Ⓐ a bird's nest in a tree
- Ⓑ a beehive in a dead, hollow log
- Ⓒ a bear's den inside an existing cave
- Ⓓ a beaver's lodge created by a dam across a river

9 Several animals interact with a tree. Which of these is **most likely** to harm the tree?
- Ⓐ birds that eat the fruit of the tree
- Ⓑ ants that crawl up the trunk of the tree
- Ⓒ caterpillars that eat the leaves of the tree
- Ⓓ squirrels that build nests in the trunk of the tree

GO ON

Name _____ Date _____ **Chapter 5**

Chapter Test — How Do Living Things Interact with Their Environment?

10 Which of these is a way people use the environment to meet their needs?

Ⓐ throwing litter on the ground

Ⓑ recycling wood to build homes

Ⓒ using chemicals to grow more food

Ⓓ using water behind a dam for electricity

Directions: Read the question. Then write your answer on the lines.

11 Explain one way that people affect their environment in a harmful way.

_____

_____

What is a possible solution to this problem?

_____

_____

Test Score

_____ /12

Name _____ Date _____ **Chapter 6**

Chapter Self-Assessment: How Do the Parts of an Organism Work Together?

Directions: Write a ✓ in the box to show the answer that is true for you.

	Yes	Not Yet
❶ I know that people have body parts that help them get what they need.		
❷ I know that organisms have different parts working together to help them live and grow.		
❸ I can describe the major organs of body systems and how they work.		
❹ I know that a balanced diet and regular exercise are good health habits.		
❺ I know that avoiding drugs, alcohol, and tobacco are good health habits.		
❻ I know that washing hands often is a good health habit.		

Directions: Think about the things you have studied in this chapter. Then finish the sentence.

❼ I am interested in learning more about _____

_____

_____

_____

Name _____ Date _____ Chapter 6

Chapter Test How Do the Parts of an Organism Work Together?

Directions: Read each question. Then choose the correct answer.

1 What allows people to do the many different things needed to stay alive?

Ⓐ having good exercise habits

Ⓑ having a variety of organ systems

Ⓒ having bones throughout the body

Ⓓ having a brain controlling the body

2 Systems in an animal's body help it live and grow. Which of these **best** describes a system?

Ⓐ all of an animal's body parts

Ⓑ the biggest organs in the body of an animal

Ⓒ a body part in an animal that has a special job

Ⓓ a group of an animal's organs that work together

3 Which statement is **true** about the circulatory system?

Ⓐ It carries blood all through the body.

Ⓑ It contains the heart and the lungs.

Ⓒ Arteries carry blood toward the heart.

Ⓓ The movement of veins causes a pulse.

GO ON

Name _____ Date _____

Chapter 6

Chapter Test — How Do the Parts of an Organism Work Together?

4 Which organ of the digestive system has the main job of absorbing materials the body can use?

Ⓐ mouth

Ⓑ stomach

Ⓒ intestines

Ⓓ esophagus

5 Look at the picture. Which of these describes what this system does in the body?

Ⓐ It gives shape and support to the body.

Ⓑ It causes the heart to pump blood in the body.

Ⓒ It uses nerves to send information to the brain.

Ⓓ It breaks up food into small pieces for the stomach.

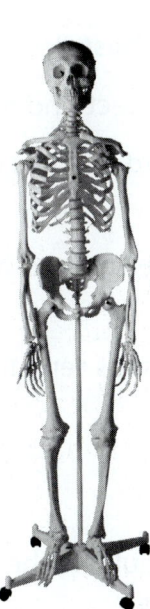

GO ON

Name _____ Date _____

Chapter Test — **How Do the Parts of an Organism Work Together?**

Chapter 6

6 Which organ is part of the respiratory system?

- Ⓐ heart
- Ⓑ lungs
- Ⓒ brain
- Ⓓ muscle

7 Which statement **best** describes how the nervous system works?

- Ⓐ The bones protect and tell the organs how to move throughout the body.
- Ⓑ The spinal cord absorbs nutrients to send throughout the body through the nerves.
- Ⓒ The brain receives messages through the senses and then tells the body what to do.
- Ⓓ The blood vessels send messages about the environment to different parts of the body.

8 Which activity would be the **most** helpful for a 10-year-old person to stay healthy?

- Ⓐ exercising once a month
- Ⓑ sleeping seven hours a night
- Ⓒ eating different kinds of foods
- Ⓓ watching an hour of television each day

Name _____ Date _____

Chapter 6

Chapter Test — How Do the Parts of an Organism Work Together?

9 Some of Elizabeth's friends have a cold. Elizabeth does not want to get sick. What is the **best** way for her to protect herself from germs?

Ⓐ washing her hands

Ⓑ eating a large lunch

Ⓒ staying away from alcohol

Ⓓ sharing her lunch with her friends

Directions: Read the question. Then write your answer on the lines.

10 Some muscle movements can be controlled, and others are automatic.

Write one example of a controlled muscle movement.

_____

_____

Write one example of an automatic muscle movement.

_____

_____

Test Score

_____ /11

Grade 4 Life Science

Life Science Benchmark Test

Life Science Benchmark Test 38

Benchmark Test

Purpose and Description

A Benchmark Test is available for the Life Science Unit. The Benchmark Test uses multiple-choice and short constructed-response items to measure student understanding of the Life Science concepts taught in this unit.

Administering the Test

Administer the Benchmark Test after evaluating the results of all the Chapter Tests and presenting any additional instruction if needed. Allow about 30 minutes for administration. Make a copy of the test for each student.

All directions may be read to the students. All test items, including any charts and diagrams, may be read to students if deemed necessary. Use a copy of the test to point out directions, test items, and response areas.

Introduce the test by telling students the purpose of the test.

- To begin the test, read the directions.
- Tell students how they are expected to respond to that type of item, for example, by filling in a circle.
- Give students time to work individually on the test, and allow a reasonable amount of time for them to complete it.
- Look to see that students are responding to the items in the correct manner.
- Read the directions and items in the test as necessary, explaining to students how they are expected to respond to any new item formats.

Students may not use their books during the test.

Scoring the Tests and Using the Results

Score the Benchmark Test with the Answer Key on page 146. Use the Student Profile on page 147 to determine if students need additional instruction in any of the science concepts presented. For more information on scoring, see page 133.

Name _____ Date _____

Benchmark Test — Life Science

Directions: Read each question. Then choose the correct answer.

1 Which of these makes food out of sunlight, water, and air?

Ⓐ predators

Ⓑ producers

Ⓒ consumers

Ⓓ decomposers

2 Why are honeybees important to flowering plants?

Ⓐ They help with pollination.

Ⓑ They perform photosynthesis.

Ⓒ They provide food for the plants.

Ⓓ They carry their seeds to new areas.

3 The life cycles of conifers and flowering plants both include seeds that

Ⓐ grow into spores.

Ⓑ are pollinated by insects.

Ⓒ can reproduce using fruits.

Ⓓ germinate and grow into adult plants.

Benchmark Test: Life Science

4 Which of these **best** describes an example of seed dispersal?
  Ⓐ A hummingbird carries pollen.
  Ⓑ A bee drinks nectar from a lily.
  Ⓒ A pollen tube grows to the ovary.
  Ⓓ A breeze blows on a dandelion flower.

5 When a cricket hatches out of its egg, it looks like a tiny version of an adult cricket. Then it grows and eventually becomes adult-sized. What stage is the cricket in just after it hatches?
  Ⓐ pupa
  Ⓑ larva
  Ⓒ adult
  Ⓓ nymph

6 A cat's fur color is a result of heredity. A cat has kittens with black fur. How did the kittens **most likely** get this fur color?
  Ⓐ The black fur was passed on to the kittens from the kittens' parents.
  Ⓑ The food that the mother cat ate caused the kittens' fur to be black.
  Ⓒ The temperature when they were born caused the kittens' fur to be black.
  Ⓓ The kittens' black fur was determined by the environment the mother cat lived in.

7 Which of these is **most likely** an example of an acquired trait?
  Ⓐ a scar on a goat's face
  Ⓑ the size of an alligator's head
  Ⓒ a curve in an elephant's tusks
  Ⓓ the way a spider weaves its web

8 Which group makes up a community?
  Ⓐ water, fish, algae
  Ⓑ sun, frogs, cattails
  Ⓒ soil, turtles, dandelions
  Ⓓ leopard, panda, bamboo

9 Which statement about conifers is **true**?
  Ⓐ They grow fruit.
  Ⓑ They have petals.
  Ⓒ They have cones.
  Ⓓ They grow spores.

GO ON

Name _____ Date _____

Benchmark Test — Life Science

10 Which of these shows how energy passes from one living thing to another?

Ⓐ an herbivore eats a carnivore

Ⓑ a producer eats an herbivore

Ⓒ a carnivore eats an omnivore

Ⓓ a producer eats an omnivore

11 Lions are a zebra's predator. What will **most likely** happen to zebras if the population of lions decreases?

Ⓐ There will be fewer zebras.

Ⓑ The zebras will increase in number.

Ⓒ The zebras will disappear completely.

Ⓓ There will be the same number of zebras.

12 Look at the picture of two wolves below.

Which of these **best** explains the wolves' behavior?

Ⓐ They are playing with each other.

Ⓑ They are exercising their muscles.

Ⓒ They are competing for a resource.

Ⓓ They are making their own food.

Benchmark Test: Life Science

13 The shape of the bird's beak is an adaptation. What is the **most likely** reason the shape of this bird's beak is important?

- Ⓐ It lets the bird move to new locations.
- Ⓑ It allows the bird to camouflage itself.
- Ⓒ It lets the bird watch out for nearby predators.
- Ⓓ It allows the bird to eat a particular type of food.

14 Which of these **best** describes when an animal will know to hunt for food?

- Ⓐ when it senses a predator is nearby
- Ⓑ after the sun rises each day
- Ⓒ after it has a full drink of water
- Ⓓ when its body lets it know it is hungry

15 A scientist finds a fossil of a fish in a desert. This **most likely** tells the scientist that

- Ⓐ the area used to be underwater.
- Ⓑ the fish and its relatives are extinct.
- Ⓒ the area has always been hot and dry.
- Ⓓ the fish sometimes moved on dry land.

Name _____   Date _____

Benchmark Test — Life Science

16 Which of these is the **best** example of how a plant changes the environment around it?

- Ⓐ A pine tree produces seeds.
- Ⓑ An oak tree's roots split a rock.
- Ⓒ An apple tree's leaves change color.
- Ⓓ A tree grows taller to reach more sunlight.

17 Which of these is the **best** example of how a plant adapts to seasonal changes in the northern United States?

- Ⓐ Grasses bloom in the fall.
- Ⓑ Oak trees grow taller in the winter.
- Ⓒ Roses change color in the summer.
- Ⓓ Maple trees grow new leaves in the spring.

18 Which of these **best** describes how an animal might adapt to the coming winter?

- Ⓐ A deer will shed some of its fur.
- Ⓑ A goose will fly to a warmer location.
- Ⓒ A snowshoe hare's fur will turn brown.
- Ⓓ A woodchuck will wake from hibernation.

GO ON

Name _____ Date _____

Benchmark Test Life Science

19 Which of these is a way that humans can **help** the environment?

Ⓐ They use trees from a forest to build houses.

Ⓑ They cause pollution by using coal and gas.

Ⓒ They make fish ladders so salmon can swim upstream.

Ⓓ They put chemicals on crops to control weeds and insects.

20 Which of these **best** describes how the human body gets the nutrients it needs?

Ⓐ The blood carries the food and its nutrients around the body.

Ⓑ The organs of the respiratory system get the nutrients out of the food.

Ⓒ The brain takes the nutrients from food and sends them around the body.

Ⓓ The organs of the digestive system break down food and absorb its nutrients.

21 Ashley wants to develop good health habits. What would be the **best** way for her to keep her body healthy?

Ⓐ Eat a lot of food.

Ⓑ Exercise every day.

Ⓒ Exercise once a week.

Ⓓ Eat mainly bread and meat.

Name _____ Date _____

Benchmark Test   Life Science

Directions: Read each question. Then write your answers on the lines.

22 Jeremy is studying the parts that a rose bush and a pine tree use to reproduce. How are these parts different?

_____

_____

How are they similar?

_____

_____

23 How are the babies of a sea turtle and butterfly similar?

_____

_____

How are they different?

_____

_____

Test Score

_____ /25

DONE!

Grade 4 Life Science

Earth Science Chapter Tests and Self-Assessments

> Chapter 1: How Do Earth and Its Moon Move? 47
> Chapter 2: How Are Rocks Alike and Different? 53
> Chapter 3: What Are Renewable and Nonrenewable Resources?...59
> Chapter 4: How Do Slow Processes Change Earth's Surface? 66
> Chapter 5: What Changes Do Volcanoes and Earthquakes Cause? 71
> Chapter 6: What Can We Observe About Weather? 76

Chapter Self-Assessment

Purpose and Description

The Chapter Self-Assessment helps students review their own progress toward meeting specific learning objectives in the chapter. Students also indicate an area of interest for further study. Make a copy of the Chapter Self-Assessment for each student and have them fill it out before taking the Chapter Test.

Chapter Tests

Purpose and Description

A Chapter Test is available for each of the six chapters in the Earth Science Unit. Each Chapter Test is designed to check student progress on the specific instruction within the chapter and to provide an early indicator that additional instruction may be necessary. Chapter Tests generally use multiple-choice and short constructed-response items to measure student understanding of the Earth Science concepts taught in this unit.

Administering the Tests

Administer the test for each chapter after instruction. Allow 10 to 20 minutes for administration, depending on the length of the test. Make a copy of the test for each student.

All directions may be read to the students. All test items, including any charts and diagrams, may be read to students if deemed necessary. Use a copy of the test to point out directions, test items, and response areas.

Introduce the test by telling students the purpose of the test.

- To begin the test, read the directions.
- Tell students how they are expected to respond to that type of item, for example, by filling in a circle.

Earth Science Chapter Tests and Self-Assessments

- Give students time to work individually on the test, and allow a reasonable amount of time for them to complete it.
- Look to see that students are responding to the items in the correct manner.
- Read the directions and items in the test as necessary, explaining to students how they are expected to respond to any new item formats.

Students may not use their books during the test.

Scoring the Tests and Using the Results

Score the Chapter Tests with the Answer Keys in the Scoring and Reporting Tools section, beginning on page 134. Use the Student Profiles in the same section to determine if students need additional instruction in any of the science concepts presented. For more information on scoring, see page 133.

Name _____ Date _____ **Chapter 1**

Chapter Self-Assessment — How Do Earth and Its Moon Move?

Directions: Write a ✓ in the box to show the answer that is true for you.

	Yes	Not Yet
❶ I can compare data about the sun, moon, and Earth.		
❷ I can describe the apparent movement of the sun and moon across the sky.		
❸ I can explain that Earth is tilted on its axis.		
❹ I can explain that Earth's movement and position cause the seasons.		
❺ I can explain the motion of the moon around Earth.		
❻ I can explain how the shape of the moon follows a pattern that repeats itself.		

Directions: Think about the things you have studied in this chapter. Then finish the sentence.

❼ I am interested in learning more about _____

_____

_____

_____

Grade 4 Assessment

Name _____ Date _____   **Chapter 1**

Chapter Test: How Do Earth and Its Moon Move?

Directions: Read each question. Then choose the correct answer.

1 Mary is making observations about the sun. Which of these could be observations that Mary makes?

- Ⓐ It is early in the morning. The sun seems to be moving in the eastern sky.
- Ⓑ It is still dark. The sun seems to be rising from the west.
- Ⓒ It is noon. The sun is low in the western sky.
- Ⓓ It is after sunset. The sun is overhead.

2 Sarah observes the star pattern Orion for several months. She notices that the star pattern Orion appears to move across the sky. Why is this?

- Ⓐ As the stars orbit the sun, the star patterns move.
- Ⓑ As Earth rotates, the stars in Orion appear to rotate.
- Ⓒ As the stars move around Earth, their patterns change.
- Ⓓ As Earth revolves around the sun, its position in space changes.

3 Which comparison of the sun, moon, and Earth is correct?

- Ⓐ The sun's surface has no air; the moon and Earth both have air.
- Ⓑ The sun's surface includes liquid rock; the moon and Earth both have solid rock.
- Ⓒ The sun's surface contains no liquid water; the moon and Earth both have liquid water.
- Ⓓ The sun's surface is made up of hot gases; the moon and Earth both have rock surfaces.

GO ON

Name _____ Date _____

Chapter 1

Chapter Test — How Do Earth and Its Moon Move?

4 Which statement **best** describes the effect of Earth's rotation?

Ⓐ Seasons change.

Ⓑ Star patterns move.

Ⓒ Night and day occur.

Ⓓ The moon has phases.

5 Which statement **best** explains why there are seasons on Earth?

Ⓐ Earth rotates on its axis.

Ⓑ Earth is tilted on its axis.

Ⓒ Earth is closer to the sun in summer.

Ⓓ Earth's sky becomes cloudy in winter.

6 Which motion takes about 365 days to complete?

Ⓐ Earth rotating on its axis

Ⓑ the sun revolving around Earth

Ⓒ Earth revolving around the sun

Ⓓ the moon revolving around Earth

7 Which of these can be seen most nights of the year in the night sky?

Ⓐ the sun

Ⓑ the moon

Ⓒ spacecraft

Ⓓ the star pattern Lyra

8 Why does the United States experience summer in June?

Ⓐ The Northern Hemisphere is tilted toward the sun in June.

Ⓑ The Northern Hemisphere has a higher latitude in June.

Ⓒ Earth is closest to the sun in June.

Ⓓ Earth's axis tilts more in June.

GO ON

Grade 4 Earth Science

Chapter Test — How Do Earth and Its Moon Move?

9 Why is winter more mild at the Equator than at the mid-latitudes?

Ⓐ The Equator is closer to the sun than the mid-latitudes are.

Ⓑ The seasons at the Equator are opposite what they are in the mid-latitudes.

Ⓒ The Equator always gets direct sun, while the mid-latitudes are cooler when they are tilted away from the sun.

Ⓓ The sun shines all day and night at the Equator, while the sun sets in the late afternoon during winter in the mid-latitudes.

10 What do the sun, moon, and stars have in common?

Ⓐ They all revolve around Earth.

Ⓑ They can be seen in Earth's sky.

Ⓒ They are all about the same size.

Ⓓ They all appear to change shape.

11 Which of these is true about the movement of the moon?

Ⓐ It revolves around the sun once a month.

Ⓑ It rotates on its axis once every 24 hours.

Ⓒ It rotates on its axis once every 365 days.

Ⓓ It revolves around Earth about every 4 weeks.

12 Which of these **best** describes the moon?

Ⓐ It has strong gravity.

Ⓑ It has hot gas in the air.

Ⓒ It has low areas and mountains.

Ⓓ It has cold temperatures day and night.

GO ON

Name _____ Date _____ Chapter 1

Chapter Test How Do Earth and Its Moon Move?

⓭ As Earth revolves around the sun, the Southern Hemisphere is sometimes pointed toward the sun, and at other times it is pointed away from the sun. What does this changing position cause?

Ⓐ seasons

Ⓑ day and night

Ⓒ the phases of the moon

Ⓓ the apparent motion of the sun

⓮ Which picture shows the phase that would appear in the night sky one week after a full moon?

Ⓐ

Ⓒ

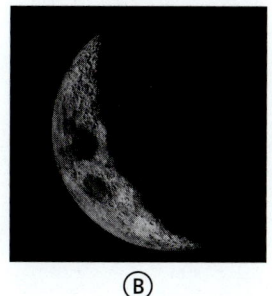
Ⓑ

Ⓓ

GO ON

Grade 4 Earth Science

Name _____ Date _____ **Chapter 1**

Chapter Test | **How Do Earth and Its Moon Move?**

Directions: Read the question. Then write your answer on the lines.

15 Roy observes the moon in the night sky. At 8 p.m., he sees that the moon is directly above the telephone pole at the end of his street. He also sees that there is a tall building to the east of the moon. Roy observes the moon again two hours later.

Where in the sky would the moon **most likely** appear at 10 p.m. compared to the position of the telephone pole and the building?

_____

_____

Why would the moon **most likely** appear in that location?

_____

_____

Test Score

_____ /16

52

Grade 4 Earth Science

Name _____ Date _____ Chapter 2

Chapter Self-Assessment — **How Are Rocks Alike and Different?**

Directions: Write a ✓ in the box to show the answer that is true for you.

	Yes	Not Yet
❶ I know that there are many different kinds of rocks.		
❷ I can define and compare the properties of rocks and minerals.		
❸ I know how technology and tools are used in science.		
❹ I can explain how igneous rock is formed and describe its properties.		
❺ I can explain how sedimentary rock is formed and describe its properties.		
❻ I can explain how metamorphic rock is formed and describe its properties.		
❼ I can explain how fossils can be used to tell about the past.		

Directions: Think about the things you have studied in this chapter. Then finish the sentence.

❽ I am interested in learning more about _____

_____

_____

_____

Name _____ Date _____

Chapter 2

Chapter Test — **How Are Rocks Alike and Different?**

Directions: Read each question. Then choose the correct answer.

1 Which process would form an igneous rock?
- Ⓐ Melted rock cools and then hardens.
- Ⓑ Small pieces of rock get squeezed together.
- Ⓒ Animal remains are covered by rock that hardens around them.
- Ⓓ Heat or pressure changes an existing piece of rock into a new rock.

2 What is a mineral?
- Ⓐ small broken-up pieces of rocks
- Ⓑ a solid, nonliving material found in nature
- Ⓒ the remains of an animal that lived in the past
- Ⓓ magma that escapes through openings in Earth's surface

3 A rock was placed under heat and pressure so that its properties changed. It is now a new type of rock. What type of rock is the new rock?
- Ⓐ fossil
- Ⓑ igneous
- Ⓒ sedimentary
- Ⓓ metamorphic

GO ON

Name _____ Date _____

Chapter 2

Chapter Test — How Are Rocks Alike and Different?

4 How can these two rocks be compared based on a **property** that can be seen?

Rock 1

Rock 2

- Ⓐ Rock 1 is magnetic. Rock 2 is not magnetic.
- Ⓑ Rock 1 has air holes. Rock 2 has no air holes.
- Ⓒ Rock 1 has minerals. Rock 2 has no minerals.
- Ⓓ Rock 1 has cleavage. Rock 2 has no cleavage.

5 How can the streak of a mineral be tested?
- Ⓐ Break it to see if the pieces are cubes or sheets.
- Ⓑ Rub it across a tile to see the color of the powder it leaves.
- Ⓒ Shine a bright light on it to see how its surface reflects light.
- Ⓓ Rub it against different things to see how easily it can be scratched.

GO ON

Name _____ Date _____ Chapter 2

Chapter Test — How Are Rocks Alike and Different?

6 Which property of minerals is measured by scratching the surface of the mineral?
- Ⓐ color
- Ⓑ luster
- Ⓒ hardness
- Ⓓ magnetism

7 Donna is trying to identify a mineral. She notes that the mineral can easily break into flat sections. What property has she observed?
- Ⓐ luster
- Ⓑ streak
- Ⓒ cleavage
- Ⓓ hardness

8 How are coal, sandstone, and granite similar?
- Ⓐ They are all rocks.
- Ⓑ They all have fossils.
- Ⓒ They are all minerals.
- Ⓓ They all have the same color.

9 Which of these is an igneous rock?
- Ⓐ a rock that formed when lava cooled
- Ⓑ a rock that formed by heat and pressure
- Ⓒ a rock that formed by plant and animal material
- Ⓓ a rock that formed when small rocks were pressed together

GO ON

Chapter Test How Are Rocks Alike and Different?

10 How does sedimentary rock form?

Ⓐ Heat causes the properties of a rock to change.

Ⓑ Pressure rearranges the mineral crystals in the rock.

Ⓒ Pieces of rock and other materials squeeze together.

Ⓓ Minerals melt deep underground and harden into rock.

11 Anna finds a rock that contains a fossil. Which type of rock does Anna **most likely** have?

Ⓐ mineral

Ⓑ igneous

Ⓒ metamorphic

Ⓓ sedimentary

12 Emily finds a fossil in a rock. Which of these would the fossil help her determine?

Ⓐ age of the rock

Ⓑ color of the rock

Ⓒ texture of the rock

Ⓓ grain size of the rock

Name _____ Date _____ **Chapter 2**

Chapter Test | **How Are Rocks Alike and Different?**

13 Slate is a dark gray metamorphic rock. Which statement **best** describes how slate forms?

Ⓐ Heat and pressure turned a sedimentary rock into slate.

Ⓑ Minerals melted deep underground and cooled into slate.

Ⓒ Pieces of dead plants decayed long ago and became slate.

Ⓓ Grains of sand and other minerals collected and hardened over time.

14 Rocks are **mostly** made of

Ⓐ dirt.

Ⓑ lava.

Ⓒ fossils.

Ⓓ minerals.

Directions: Read the question. Then write your answer on the lines.

15 Joshua wants to examine the grains in a rock. Name a tool that Joshua could use for this purpose.

_____

How will this tool help Joshua examine the grains?

_____

_____

Test Score

_____ /16

DONE!

Grade 4 Earth Science

Name _____ Date _____ **Chapter 3**

Chapter Self-Assessment — **What Are Renewable and Nonrenewable Resources?**

Directions: Write a ✓ in the box to show the answer that is true for you.

	Yes	Not Yet
❶ I can define and identify renewable natural resources.		
❷ I can define and identify nonrenewable natural resources.		
❸ I can identify and describe the properties of soil.		
❹ I can identify ways people affect Earth's natural resources.		
❺ I know ways to help the environment.		

Directions: Think about the things you have studied in this chapter. Then finish the sentence.

❻ I am interested in learning more about _____

_____

_____

_____

Name _____ Date _____   **Chapter 3**

Chapter Test What Are Renewable and Nonrenewable Resources?

Directions: Read each question. Then choose the correct answer.

1 Farmers make sure the plants they grow have soil, nutrients, water, air, and light. Which of these natural resources is a nonrenewable resource?

Ⓐ air

Ⓑ soil

Ⓒ light

Ⓓ water

2 Which of these natural resources is renewable?

Ⓐ oil

Ⓑ coal

Ⓒ metal

Ⓓ wood

3 Which of these items is a natural resource?

Ⓐ car

Ⓑ rock

Ⓒ road

Ⓓ building

Name _____ Date _____ Chapter 3

Chapter Test — **What Are Renewable and Nonrenewable Resources?**

4 Which of these resources is renewable?

- Ⓐ water
- Ⓑ coal
- Ⓒ soil
- Ⓓ oil

5 The Jones family bought cows, a tractor, some apple trees, and a barn to help start their farm. Which of these things are renewable resources?

- Ⓐ tractor and barn
- Ⓑ tractor and cows
- Ⓒ barn and apple trees
- Ⓓ cows and apple trees

6 Which pair of resources is renewable?

- Ⓐ coal and oil
- Ⓑ sunlight and air
- Ⓒ copper and iron
- Ⓓ natural gas and rocks

GO ON

Name _____ Date _____

Chapter 3

Chapter Test — **What Are Renewable and Nonrenewable Resources?**

7 Which of these materials is a nonrenewable resource?

Ⓐ rocks

Ⓑ wind

Ⓒ plants

Ⓓ sunlight

8 Which statement about metals is **true**?

Ⓐ Metals are an energy source.

Ⓑ Metals are nonrenewable resources.

Ⓒ Metals are continuously being replaced.

Ⓓ Metals are formed from the remains of living things.

9 Which statement **best** describes fossil fuels?

Ⓐ They are used to build bridges.

Ⓑ They are rocks that contain metals.

Ⓒ They are important in controlling erosion.

Ⓓ They are resources that cannot be replaced quickly.

GO ON

Name _____ Date _____ Chapter 3

Chapter Test — What Are Renewable and Nonrenewable Resources?

10 What type of resource is soil?

- Ⓐ a resource found in ores
- Ⓑ a human-made resource
- Ⓒ a nonrenewable resource
- Ⓓ a resource used to make glass

11 Which of these are components of soil?

- Ⓐ rock and oil
- Ⓑ sand and roots
- Ⓒ rock and humus
- Ⓓ humus and roots

12 Which of these is an example of conservation of Earth's natural resources?

- Ⓐ taking shorter showers
- Ⓑ building mines for copper
- Ⓒ cutting down trees to make paper
- Ⓓ using fossil fuels to power machines

Name _____ Date _____ Chapter 3

Chapter Test — **What Are Renewable and Nonrenewable Resources?**

13 Charles uses a big barrel to catch and store rain. Then he uses that rain to water his plants. How is Charles helping the environment?

Ⓐ He is polluting water.

Ⓑ He is conserving water.

Ⓒ He is using water for electricity.

Ⓓ He is using water to erode the soil.

14 Which of these is one way to conserve mineral resources?

Ⓐ using less water

Ⓑ using less fossil fuel

Ⓒ recycling aluminum cans

Ⓓ reusing plastic water bottles

15 What is one way that people can begin to use less fossil fuel?

Ⓐ wearing nylon clothes

Ⓑ composting

Ⓒ using solar power

Ⓓ using no-till farming

GO ON

Name _____ Date _____ Chapter 3

Chapter Test — What Are Renewable and Nonrenewable Resources?

Directions: Read the question. Then write your answer on the lines.

16 Describe no-till farming.

_____

_____

Why do some farmers grow plants using no-till farming?

_____

_____

_____

Test Score
_____ /17

Grade 4 Earth Science

Name _____ Date _____ Chapter 4

Chapter Self-Assessment — How Do Slow Processes Change Earth's Surface?

Directions: Write a ✓ in the box to show the answer that is true for you.

	Yes	Not Yet
❶ I know that Earth's surface can change slowly.		
❷ I can identify major landforms on Earth's surface.		
❸ I can identify and define how weathering, erosion, and deposition change Earth's surface.		
❹ I know how weathering, erosion, and deposition affect people.		

Directions: Think about the things you have studied in this chapter. Then finish the sentence.

❺ I am interested in learning more about _____

_____

_____

_____

Name _____ Date _____

Chapter 4

Chapter Test: How Do Slow Processes Change Earth's Surface?

Directions: Read each question. Then choose the correct answer.

1 Which landform is found only where land meets an ocean?

Ⓐ plain

Ⓑ valley

Ⓒ coastline

Ⓓ mountain

2 How does weathering help form a sandy beach by the ocean?

Ⓐ Melting glaciers deposit grains of sand.

Ⓑ Sandstorms deposit sand from nearby deserts.

Ⓒ Waves break rocks into pieces, making grains of sand.

Ⓓ Chemicals in the waves dissolve large rocks into sand.

3 A deep cave was discovered underground. Scientists found that the walls of the cave were made of limestone. The cave **most likely** formed through weathering by

Ⓐ glacial ice.

Ⓑ weak acid.

Ⓒ heavy wind.

Ⓓ high waves.

GO ON

Chapter Test — **How Do Slow Processes Change Earth's Surface?**

Chapter 4

4. In the desert, wind carrying sand causes abrasion to rocks. What will happen to the rocks over time?
   - Ⓐ They will crack.
   - Ⓑ They will blow away.
   - Ⓒ They will become bigger.
   - Ⓓ They will become smoother.

5. In what way is a river valley like a canyon?
   - Ⓐ Both are flat areas of land.
   - Ⓑ Both can be found near oceans.
   - Ⓒ Both are formed by moving water.
   - Ⓓ Both rise high above the land around them.

6. How do weathering and erosion cause a landslide?
   - Ⓐ Rock and soil slip downhill.
   - Ⓑ Moving ice deposits sediment.
   - Ⓒ Weak acid dissolves limestone.
   - Ⓓ Sandstorms blow sediment against rock.

7. Last winter, Julie noticed a rock in her yard that had a small crack with water in it. After winter passed, she looked again and found that the crack had changed. What **most likely** happened to the crack during the winter?
   - Ⓐ It got bigger because the water froze and expanded.
   - Ⓑ It got smaller after the water deposited sediment.
   - Ⓒ It got bigger because the water eroded the rock.
   - Ⓓ It got smaller when the water mixed with dust.

8. A group of large boulders are in the middle of a grassy field. The boulders were once far away from the field. Which of these **most likely** moved the boulders to the grassy field?
   - Ⓐ weathering and erosion by a river
   - Ⓑ erosion and deposition by a glacier
   - Ⓒ weathering and abrasion by a sinkhole
   - Ⓓ abrasion and deposition by a sandstorm

9. What is weathering?
   - Ⓐ dropping of sediment in a new place
   - Ⓑ the breaking apart or wearing away of rock
   - Ⓒ movement of sediment from one place to another
   - Ⓓ the creation and destruction of landforms by weather

GO ON

68

Grade 4 Earth Science

Name _____ Date _____ **Chapter 4**

Chapter Test: How Do Slow Processes Change Earth's Surface?

10 A sandstorm can move sand over great distances. Which **most likely** happens during a sandstorm?

- Ⓐ Sediment is deposited in a new place.
- Ⓑ Rocks and soil slide down a hillside.
- Ⓒ Water freezes and splits rocks.
- Ⓓ A cave forms underground.

11 How is a delta formed?

- Ⓐ A river carves out a delta with rushing water.
- Ⓑ Ocean waves carve out a delta with moving water.
- Ⓒ A river deposits sediment when it reaches an ocean.
- Ⓓ A glacier deposits sediment when it melts in an ocean.

12 Long Island, New York, was shaped by glaciers. Two moraines are found on Long Island. How did these moraines form?

- Ⓐ The glaciers caused erosion, which enriched the soil.
- Ⓑ As the glaciers melted away, sediment was deposited.
- Ⓒ Rocks carried in the glaciers became sharp and jagged.
- Ⓓ The ice in the glaciers caused rocks to freeze and break apart.

13 Which of these is an example of Earth's surface changing slowly over time?

- Ⓐ Waves get a little bigger each year.
- Ⓑ Wind gets a little stronger each year.
- Ⓒ Valleys get a little narrower each year.
- Ⓓ Canyons get a little deeper each year.

14 A house is built on a low cliff near an ocean. Which of these describes how erosion could **most likely** affect the house?

- Ⓐ Extra sediment could build up around the house.
- Ⓑ The soil around the house could be moved by a glacier.
- Ⓒ The paint on the house could be worn away by abrasion.
- Ⓓ Sediment that the house is standing on could be removed.

GO ON

Name _____ Date _____ **Chapter 4**

Chapter Test How Do Slow Processes Change Earth's Surface?

15 A farm near a river has very rich soil. What **most likely** caused the soil to be so rich there?

Ⓐ Wind brought the rich soil from the river.

Ⓑ Floods from the river deposited the rich soil.

Ⓒ Rain dissolved minerals to make the soil rich.

Ⓓ Plants cracked rocks into pieces to make the soil rich.

Directions: Read the question. Then write your answer on the lines.

16 Explain how water causes both erosion and deposition.

_____

_____

Test Score

_____ /17

Name _____ Date _____ **Chapter 5**

Chapter Self-Assessment — **What Changes Do Volcanoes and Earthquakes Cause?**

Directions: Write a ✓ in the box to show the answer that is true for you.

	Yes	Not Yet
❶ I know how Earth's surface can change rapidly.		
❷ I know that Earth is made of layers and that Earth's surface in divided into plates.		
❸ I know that plate movement can build mountains.		
❹ I can explain how earthquakes happen and how they can change Earth's surface.		
❺ I can explain why volcanoes happen and how they can change Earth's surface.		
❻ I can explain why landslides happen and how they can change Earth's surface.		

Directions: Think about the things you have studied in this chapter. Then finish the sentence.

❼ I am interested in learning more about _____

_____

_____

_____

Name _____ Date _____

Chapter 5

Chapter Test — **What Changes Do Volcanoes and Earthquakes Cause?**

Directions: Read each question. Then choose the correct answer.

1 Which statement is **true** about the structure of Earth?
- Ⓐ Earth is made up of several layers.
- Ⓑ Earth's surface always stays the same.
- Ⓒ Earth's surface is a solid sheet of rock.
- Ⓓ Earth is all liquid rock under the surface.

2 Rachel learned that the area where a mountain stands today used to be flat land. What **most likely** caused the mountain to form?
- Ⓐ Ash fell from a volcano.
- Ⓑ Wind deposited soil and rocks.
- Ⓒ Two plates pushed against each other.
- Ⓓ Gravity caused rocks and soil to move.

3 Which of these causes an earthquake?
- Ⓐ lava hardening into rock
- Ⓑ rock and soil sliding downhill
- Ⓒ rocks crashing into the ground
- Ⓓ two plates sliding past each other

GO ON

Name _____ Date _____ **Chapter 5**

Chapter Test — **What Changes Do Volcanoes and Earthquakes Cause?**

4 Mr. Wayne showed his class a picture of a large crack in the land. What **most likely** caused this crack?

- Ⓐ a landslide
- Ⓑ an earthquake
- Ⓒ a volcanic eruption
- Ⓓ molten underground rock

5 Some areas in the world have many volcanoes. What do these places **most likely** have in common?

- Ⓐ They are in places where Earth's core is cracked beneath them.
- Ⓑ They are in areas where one plate slides underneath another.
- Ⓒ They are islands built up from the floor of the ocean.
- Ⓓ They are on land that has a lot of rocks and soil.

6 Each year an island near Hawaii gets a little larger. How does this **most likely** happen?

- Ⓐ Landslides cause rocks to fall on the island.
- Ⓑ Earthquakes raise the land around the island.
- Ⓒ Volcanic eruptions add lava that builds up the land.
- Ⓓ One plate slides under and pushes up another plate.

Name _____ Date _____

Chapter 5

Chapter Test — What Changes Do Volcanoes and Earthquakes Cause?

7 A mountain town has had many landslides. Which of these most likely caused the landslides?

Ⓐ volcanic eruptions

Ⓑ snow storms

Ⓒ rain showers

Ⓓ forest fires

Directions: Read the question. Then write your answer on the lines.

8 Name one event that can cause Earth's surface to change quickly.

_____

Describe how Earth's surface would look after this change happened.

_____

_____

Test Score

_____ /9

74

Grade 4 Earth Science

Name _____ Date _____ **Chapter 6**

| **Chapter Self-Assessment** | **What Can We Observe About Weather?** |

Directions: Write a ✓ in the box to show the answer that is true for you.

	Yes	Not Yet
1 I know that air surrounds us and takes up space.		
2 I can describe the layers of the atmosphere.		
3 I can describe temperature, precipitation, air pressure, wind, and humidity and know they can be measured.		
4 I can describe how water exists in the air and how clouds form.		
5 I can describe cumulus, stratus, and cirrus clouds.		
6 I can describe how air masses, cold fronts, and warm fronts affect weather.		
7 I can identify and describe weather patterns that affect the United States.		

Directions: Think about the things you have studied in this chapter. Then finish the sentence.

8 I am interested in learning more about _____

_____

_____

_____

Name _____ Date _____ Chapter 6

Chapter Test — What Can We Observe About Weather?

Directions: Read each question. Then choose the correct answer.

1 What is true about the air in Earth's atmosphere?
- Ⓐ It keeps the entire planet cool.
- Ⓑ It surrounds people and takes up space.
- Ⓒ It is below the layer where weather occurs.
- Ⓓ It is made up mostly of oxygen and water vapor.

2 In which layer of the atmosphere is ozone found?
- Ⓐ the outer layer closest to space
- Ⓑ the layer closest to Earth's surface
- Ⓒ the second layer from Earth's surface
- Ⓓ the layer with the coldest temperatures

3 What is the **best** way to find out if a summer has been drier than usual?
- Ⓐ keep a calendar and mark the days when it rains
- Ⓑ walk outside each day to see whether the air feels dry
- Ⓒ check each morning to see if there is dew on the grass or tree leaves
- Ⓓ measure the amount of rainfall and compare it to rainfall in past summers

4 How do scientists observe air pressure?
- Ⓐ They can see it in the air.
- Ⓑ They can measure it with a barometer.
- Ⓒ They can see it move with a cold front.
- Ⓓ They can measure it with an anemometer.

GO ON

Grade 4 Earth Science

Name _____ Date _____

Chapter 6

Chapter Test | **What Can We Observe About Weather?**

5 What is humidity?

Ⓐ how warm or cold the air is

Ⓑ the process that forms clouds

Ⓒ the amount of water vapor in the air

Ⓓ the area where two air masses meet

6 When water evaporates, it becomes water vapor. What happens when water vapor condenses in the air?

Ⓐ The water vapor turns into a gas.

Ⓑ The water vapor forms clouds.

Ⓒ Dew forms and falls.

Ⓓ Humidity drops.

7 A morning is clear and warm. Fluffy clouds begin to form in the sky. What type of clouds are **most likely** forming?

Ⓐ cirrus

Ⓑ stratus

Ⓒ cumulus

Ⓓ cumulonimbus

Chapter Test — What Can We Observe About Weather?

8 What is the **best** way to describe stratus clouds?

Ⓐ low and gray

Ⓑ thick and flat

Ⓒ high, white, and thin

Ⓓ white and tall, with gray bottoms

9 What type of cloud does this picture show?

Ⓐ cirrus

Ⓑ thunderhead

Ⓒ cumulus

Ⓓ nimbostratus

10 A town's weather is cool and rainy. What kind of air mass is **most likely** causing this weather?

Ⓐ hot and dry

Ⓑ cold and dry

Ⓒ hot and humid

Ⓓ cold and humid

Name _____ Date _____ **Chapter 6**

Chapter Test What Can We Observe About Weather?

11 A cold front is moving into an area. How will the weather there **most likely** change?

Ⓐ It will be more humid.

Ⓑ There will be clear skies.

Ⓒ There will be strong storms.

Ⓓ It will be cloudy for many days.

12 For two days, the weather has been wet and rainy. The temperature has gone up. What has **most likely** happened?

Ⓐ A warm air mass has run into a cold air mass.

Ⓑ A cold air mass has run into a warm air mass.

Ⓒ Two cold air masses have run into each other.

Ⓓ Two warm air masses have run into each other.

Name _____ Date _____ **Chapter 6**

Chapter Test — What Can We Observe About Weather?

13 What type of weather will this air mass **most likely** bring to the northwestern United States?

- Ⓐ hot and dry
- Ⓑ hot and wet
- Ⓒ cold and dry
- Ⓓ cold and wet

Directions: Read the question. Then write your answer on the lines.

14 Today is sunny but cool. Tomorrow, a snowstorm is predicted. What will probably happen to the temperature between today and tomorrow?

_____

What will probably happen to the air pressure between today and tomorrow?

_____

Test Score _____ /15

Earth Science Benchmark Test

Earth Science Benchmark Test.....................................84

Benchmark Test

Purpose and Description

A Benchmark Test is available for the Earth Science Unit. The Benchmark Test uses multiple-choice and short constructed-response items to measure student understanding of the Earth Science concepts taught in this unit.

Administering the Test

Administer the Benchmark Test after evaluating the results of all the Chapter Tests and presenting any additional instruction if needed. Allow about 30 minutes for administration. Make a copy of the test for each student.

All directions may be read to the students. All test items, including any charts and diagrams, may be read to students if deemed necessary. Use a copy of the test to point out directions, test items, and response areas.

Introduce the test by telling students the purpose of the test.

- To begin the test, read the directions.
- Tell students how they are expected to respond to that type of item, for example, by filling in a circle.
- Give students time to work individually on the test, and allow a reasonable amount of time for them to complete it.
- Look to see that students are responding to the items in the correct manner.
- Read the directions and items in the test as necessary, explaining to students how they are expected to respond to any new item formats.

Students may not use their books during the test.

Scoring the Tests and Using the Results

Score the Benchmark Test with the Answer Key on page 161. Use the Student Profile on page 162 to determine if students need additional instruction in any of the science concepts presented. For more information on scoring, see page 133.

Name _____ Date _____

Benchmark Test — Earth Science

Directions: Read each question. Then choose the correct answer.

1 Which of these is a renewable resource?

- Ⓐ oil
- Ⓑ coal
- Ⓒ metal
- Ⓓ wood

2 Which of these is in order from **biggest** to **smallest**?

- Ⓐ sun, Earth, moon
- Ⓑ moon, Earth, sun
- Ⓒ Earth, sun, moon
- Ⓓ sun, moon, Earth

3 How long does Earth take to revolve around the sun?

- Ⓐ about a year
- Ⓑ about 24 days
- Ⓒ about a month
- Ⓓ about 24 hours

GO ON

Grade 4 Earth Science

Benchmark Test: Earth Science

4 Why are the months of December and January colder in the Northern Hemisphere?

Ⓐ because Earth's axis is tilted toward the moon
Ⓑ because Earth's axis is tilted away from the sun
Ⓒ because Earth's orbit around the sun has changed
Ⓓ because Earth is at the furthest point in its orbit from the sun

5 Which statement **best** describes the motion of Earth and the moon?

Ⓐ Earth rotates around the moon.
Ⓑ The moon rotates around Earth.
Ⓒ Earth revolves around the moon.
Ⓓ The moon revolves around Earth.

6 Karen wants to classify these two rocks just by looking at the pictures below. What property can she use to classify the rocks from the pictures?

Ⓐ hardness
Ⓑ grain size
Ⓒ magnetism
Ⓓ streak color

Benchmark Test: Earth Science

7 What property of minerals could **most likely** be tested using a paper clip?

Ⓐ color

Ⓑ luster

Ⓒ streak

Ⓓ magnetism

8 A scientist finds two fossils in different layers of some sedimentary rock.

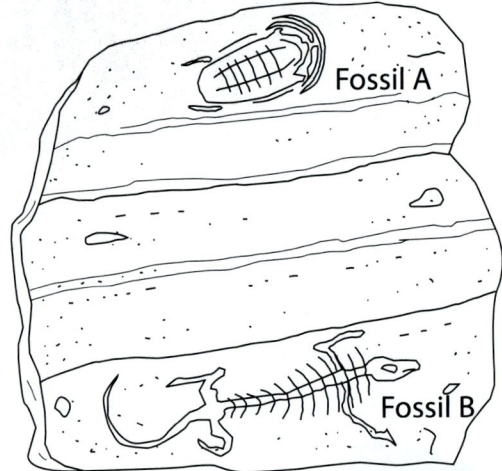

Which is the **best** conclusion the scientist can make about these fossils?

Ⓐ Fossil A is older because it was deposited near the top surface of the rock.

Ⓑ Both fossils are the same age because they are both in sedimentary rock.

Ⓒ Both fossils are the same age because they both used to live in water.

Ⓓ Fossil B is older because it was deposited in a lower layer of the rock.

Name _____ Date _____

Benchmark Test Earth Science

9 Which part of a forest is nonrenewable?

Ⓐ soil

Ⓑ wood

Ⓒ water

Ⓓ animals

10 Which of these are the main parts of soil?

Ⓐ rocks and sand

Ⓑ humus and rocks

Ⓒ roots and dead plants

Ⓓ sand and minerals

11 What is one human action that will waste water?

Ⓐ taking shorter showers

Ⓑ letting a leaky faucet drip

Ⓒ watering the lawn less often

Ⓓ running the dishwasher only when it is full

12 Which landform exists only at places where land meets an ocean?

Ⓐ plain

Ⓑ canyon

Ⓒ coastline

Ⓓ mountain

GO ON

Benchmark Test: Earth Science

13 Which of these **best** describes the result from weathering by a fast-moving river?

Ⓐ rocks with large cracks

Ⓑ smooth, rounded rocks

Ⓒ rocks with jagged edges

Ⓓ large rocks carried from different places

14 Which statement **best** describes an example of erosion?

Ⓐ Waves pick up sand and carry it away, causing a beach to get smaller.

Ⓑ Water freezes within a section of a rock and causes the rock to break apart.

Ⓒ A tree root grows along the surface of the ground and widens a crack in the ground.

Ⓓ The wind causes abrasion of a rock by blowing sediment against it.

15 How can weathering, erosion, and deposition **most** help people?

Ⓐ It can cause soil to form.

Ⓑ It can cause a landslide.

Ⓒ It can cause caves to fall in.

Ⓓ It can cause a beach to change shape.

16 Which of these is the **best** way to describe the motion of Earth and the moon through space?

Ⓐ Earth rotates around the moon, and the moon rotates around the sun.

Ⓑ Earth rotates around the moon, and the moon revolves around the sun.

Ⓒ Earth revolves around the sun, and the moon rotates around Earth.

Ⓓ Earth revolves around the sun, and the moon revolves around Earth.

Name _____ Date _____

Benchmark Test — Earth Science

17 Which statement **best** describes Earth?

Ⓐ It is solid rock all the way through.

Ⓑ It is mostly solid metal, with a hot liquid core.

Ⓒ It has a thin outer crust, a liquid middle layer, and a solid core.

Ⓓ It has a thin outer crust, solid rock middle layer, and a liquid metal core.

18 How can an earthquake change Earth's surface?

Ⓐ It can help to form soil.

Ⓑ It can cause new islands to form.

Ⓒ It can change the course of a river.

Ⓓ It can cover the land with ash and hot lava.

19 Which change on Earth's surface can be caused by a volcano?

Ⓐ the flooding of a river

Ⓑ the raising and lowering of land

Ⓒ the formation of cracks in a rock

Ⓓ the change in the shape of a hill

GO ON

Name _____ Date _____

Benchmark Test | Earth Science

20 Scientists use an anemometer to measure one of the properties of weather. What property does the anemometer measure?

Ⓐ humidity

Ⓑ wind speed

Ⓒ air pressure

Ⓓ temperature

21 Jim wants to show that air takes up space. How can he **best** do this?

Ⓐ use a hygrometer

Ⓑ stand outside on a breezy day

Ⓒ put a wind vane on top of his house

Ⓓ put a paper cup upside down in water

Name _____ Date _____

Benchmark Test — Earth Science

Directions: Read each question. Then write your answers on the lines.

22 In what form does water exist in the air?

_____

_____

What changes does this water go through when a cloud forms?

_____

_____

23 What is one example of how Earth's surface can change quickly?

_____

Explain what causes this change to occur.

_____

_____

_____

Test Score ____ /25

Physical Science Chapter Tests and Self-Assessments

> Chapter 1: How Can You Describe and Measure Properties of Matter? 95
> Chapter 2: What Are Physical and Chemical Changes? 102
> Chapter 3: How Do Forces Act? 105
> Chapter 4: What Is Magnetism? 109
> Chapter 5: What Are Some Forms of Energy?.....................112
> Chapter 6: What Is Sound? 116
> Chapter 7: What Is Electricity? 119

Chapter Self-Assessment

Purpose and Description
The Chapter Self-Assessment helps students review their own progress toward meeting specific learning objectives in the chapter. Students also indicate an area of interest for further study. Make a copy of the Chapter Self-Assessment for each student and have them fill it out before taking the Chapter Test.

Chapter Tests

Purpose and Description
A Chapter Test is available for each of the seven chapters in the Physical Science Unit. Each Chapter Test is designed to check student progress on the specific instruction within the chapter and to provide an early indicator that additional instruction may be necessary. Chapter Tests generally use multiple-choice and short constructed-response items to measure student understanding of the Physical Science concepts taught in this unit.

Administering the Tests
Administer the test for each chapter after instruction. Allow 10 to 20 minutes for administration, depending on the length of the test. Make a copy of the test for each student.

All directions may be read to the students. All test items, including any charts and diagrams, may be read to students if deemed necessary. Use a copy of the test to point out directions, test items, and response areas.

Introduce the test by telling students the purpose of the test.

- To begin the test, read the directions.
- Tell students how they are expected to respond to that type of item, for example, by filling in a circle.

Physical Science Chapter Tests and Self-Assessments

- Give students time to work individually on the test, and allow a reasonable amount of time for them to complete it.

- Look to see that students are responding to the items in the correct manner.

- Read the directions and items in the test as necessary, explaining to students how they are expected to respond to any new item formats.

Students may not use their books during the test.

Scoring the Tests and Using the Results

Score the Chapter Tests with the Answer Keys in the Scoring and Reporting Tools section, beginning on page 134. Use the Student Profiles in the same section to determine if students need additional instruction in any of the science concepts presented. For more information on scoring, see page 133.

Name _____ Date _____ **Chapter 1**

Chapter Self-Assessment — How Can You Describe and Measure Properties of Matter?

Directions: Write a ✓ in the box to show the answer that is true for you.

	Yes	Not Yet
❶ I know that all objects and substances in the world are made of matter.		
❷ I know that matter has properties that can be observed through the senses.		
❸ I know that matter takes up space and has mass.		
❹ I know that mixtures are made by combining solids or liquids or both.		
❺ I can tell the difference between the parts in a mixture or solution.		
❻ I know that water can dissolve some materials.		
❼ I know that weight is measured using a spring scale and mass is measured using a balance.		
❽ I know that the total mass of a material stays the same even if it is broken into pieces.		
❾ I know that the total mass of a material stays the same even if it changes state.		
❿ I can compare the volumes of objects.		

Directions: Think about the things you have studied in this chapter. Then finish the sentence.

⓫ I am interested in learning more about _____

_____

_____

_____

Name _____ Date _____ **Chapter 1**

Chapter Test | **How Can You Describe and Measure Properties of Matter?**

Directions: Read each question. Then choose the correct answer.

1 Heather wants to buy apples at the store. She wants dark red apples that are firm, not soft. Which of her body parts will Heather use to choose these apples?

Ⓐ her eyes and her nose
Ⓑ her eyes and her hand
Ⓒ her nose and her hand
Ⓓ her hand and her mouth

2 What do a glass of ice water, a salad, and a wooden table have in common?

Ⓐ They are all solids.
Ⓑ They are all matter.
Ⓒ They are all mixtures.
Ⓓ They are all solutions.

3 What is one way to describe **all** matter?

Ⓐ It has mass.
Ⓑ It it is a mixture.
Ⓒ It has a definite shape.
Ⓓ It is attracted to magnets.

4 There are two metal chairs in a classroom. What is true about the chairs?

Ⓐ The chairs cannot be the same color.
Ⓑ The chairs cannot be attracted to magnets.
Ⓒ The chairs cannot have the same size or mass.
Ⓓ The chairs cannot be in the same place at the same time.

GO ON

Name _____ Date _____

Chapter 1

Chapter Test — How Can You Describe and Measure Properties of Matter?

5 Nicole puts some strawberry ice cream in the freezer for three hours. She then leaves the ice cream out in the sun for three hours. What property of the ice cream will **most likely** stay the same?

- Ⓐ color
- Ⓑ shape
- Ⓒ texture
- Ⓓ hardness

6 A scientist wants to look at the texture of a material. She cannot see the details by just looking at the material. What would **most** help the scientist see the texture of the material?

- Ⓐ using a balance to determine the mass of the material
- Ⓑ using a hand lens to observe the details in the material
- Ⓒ using a magnet to see if the material is attracted to it
- Ⓓ using a ruler to measure the details in the material

7 What is the **best** tool for measuring mass?

- Ⓐ ruler
- Ⓑ beaker
- Ⓒ balance
- Ⓓ spring scale

GO ON

Name _____ Date _____ **Chapter 1**

Chapter Test — How Can You Describe and Measure Properties of Matter?

8 Which of these mixtures is made of only solids?

- Ⓐ cooked oatmeal
- Ⓑ chocolate milk
- Ⓒ pizza toppings
- Ⓓ salad dressing

9 Michael has a mixture of dirt, marbles, and water. What would be the **best** way to separate marbles from this mixture?

- Ⓐ let the mixture dry
- Ⓑ put the mixture in the freezer
- Ⓒ hold a magnet near the mixture
- Ⓓ pour the mixture through a strainer

10 A bowl contains salt, pennies, and rocks. Tom pours water into the bowl. What will **most likely** happen?

- Ⓐ Only the salt dissolves in the water.
- Ⓑ Nothing in the bowl dissolves in the water.
- Ⓒ Only the salt and rocks dissolve in the water.
- Ⓓ Everything in the bowl dissolves in the water.

GO ON

Name _____ Date _____

Chapter 1

Chapter Test: How Can You Describe and Measure Properties of Matter?

11 What unit can be used to measure the volume of a liquid?

Ⓐ liters

Ⓑ grams

Ⓒ meters

Ⓓ inches

12 Ben adds water to dirt to make mud. What is the **best** way to describe the mud?

Ⓐ It is a solid.

Ⓑ It is a liquid.

Ⓒ It is a solution.

Ⓓ It is a mixture.

13 There is a rock on one side of a balance. What information does this balance provide about the rock?

Ⓐ It weighs 13 grams.

Ⓑ It weighs 13 ounces.

Ⓒ It has a mass of 13 grams.

Ⓓ It has a mass of 13 ounces.

99

Name _____ Date _____ Chapter 1

Chapter Test — How Can You Describe and Measure Properties of Matter?

14 Daniel has a lump of clay that has a mass of 400 grams. He breaks the clay into four smaller lumps. What happens to the total **mass** of all four lumps of clay?

Ⓐ The total mass increases.

Ⓑ The total mass decreases.

Ⓒ The total mass is the same.

Ⓓ The total mass is unknown.

15 Anna has a marble, a toy car, and a graduated cylinder with water in it.

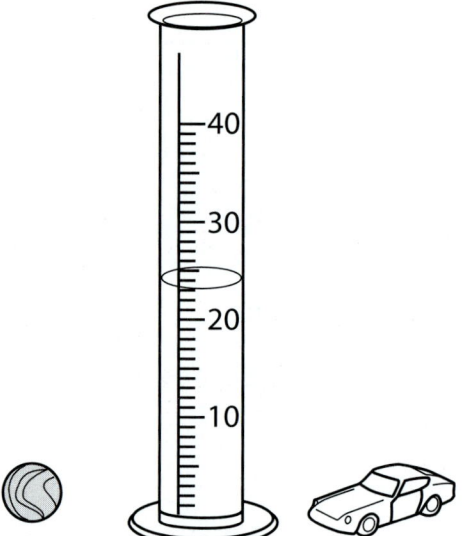

How can Anna **best** find the volume of the marble and toy car?

Ⓐ put each object in the graduated cylinder and see how much the water rises

Ⓑ pour out the water, put each object in the graduated cylinder, and see which mark it reaches

Ⓒ put both objects in the graduated cylinder, look at how much the water rises, and divide this number by two

Ⓓ put each object in a beaker, add water from the cylinder, and see how much water it took to cover the object

GO ON

100   Grade 4 Physical Science

Name _____ Date _____   Chapter 1

Chapter Test: How Can You Describe and Measure Properties of Matter?

Directions: Read the question. Then write your answer on the lines.

16 Two groups of students sorted the same six objects. Here are their results.

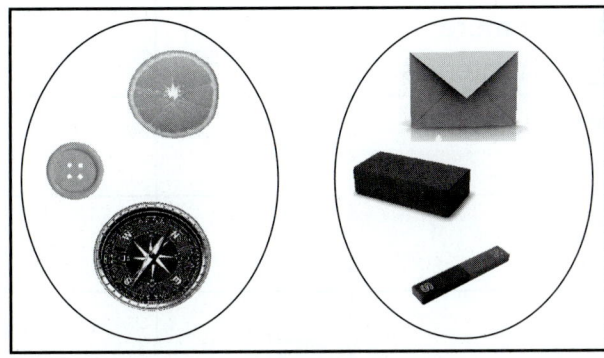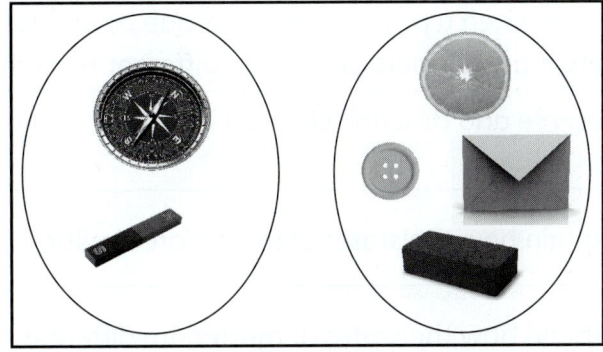

Group 1   Group 2

Why did the two groups get different results?

_____

_____

What method did each group use to sort the objects?

Group 1: _____

Group 2: _____

Test Score ____/17

101

Name _____ Date _____ Chapter 2

Chapter Self-Assessment — What Are Physical and Chemical Changes?

Directions: Write a ✓ in the box to show the answer that is true for you.

	Yes	Not Yet
❶ I can explain how matter can change from one state to another by heating and cooling.		
❷ I know that when a new material is made by combining two or more materials, it has properties that are different from the original materials.		
❸ I can observe and describe changes in the properties of materials or objects.		
❹ I can explain how the states of matter are similar.		
❺ I can explain how the states of matter are different.		
❻ I know that some properties of water make it an important resource for us.		

Directions: Think about the things you have studied in this chapter. Then finish the sentence.

❼ I am interested in learning more about _____

_____

_____

_____

Name _____ Date _____ Chapter 2

Chapter Test — **What Are Physical and Chemical Changes?**

Directions: Read each question. Then choose the correct answer.

1 Which statement is true for water in its liquid state of matter?
- Ⓐ It cannot be seen.
- Ⓑ It takes the shape of its container.
- Ⓒ It has a definite shape and volume.
- Ⓓ It has a temperature below freezing.

2 How can liquid water be changed into a gas?
- Ⓐ by rusting
- Ⓑ by cooling
- Ⓒ by heating
- Ⓓ by decaying

3 A scientist mixes two liquids together. The result is a new solid substance. Which of these is **true** about this solid?
- Ⓐ The solid can be separated back into the two liquids.
- Ⓑ The solid has different properties from the two liquids.
- Ⓒ The solid has the same state of matter as the two liquids.
- Ⓓ The solid was formed by a physical change in the two liquids.

GO ON

Name _____ Date _____ **Chapter 2**

Chapter Test | **What Are Physical and Chemical Changes?**

4 Which of these is a chemical change that happens when a piece of iron rusts?

Ⓐ It gives off heat.

Ⓑ It begins to smell bad.

Ⓒ It turns brown or black.

Ⓓ It becomes easy to break.

Directions: Read the question. Then write your answer on the lines.

5 Write two ways that the liquid and solid states of water are different.

1) _____

2) _____

Test Score

_____ /6

104

Grade 4 Physical Science

Name _____ Date _____ **Chapter 3**

Chapter Self-Assessment — How Do Forces Act?

Directions: Write a ✓ in the box to show the answer that is true for you.

	Yes	Not Yet
❶ I know that forces can be pushes or pulls.		
❷ I know that forces cause motion.		
❸ I can explain how equal and unequal forces applied to an object affect the object's movement.		
❹ I can explain that the greater the mass of an object, the greater the force needed to move that object.		
❺ I know that forces can change the direction an object moves.		
❻ I can explain that the more force you apply to an object, the more it moves.		
❼ I know that the speed of an object depends on the time it takes to go from one place to another.		
❽ I know that friction is a force that slows motion when objects are touching.		
❾ I know that gravity is a force that pulls objects toward the center of Earth.		
❿ I know that weight is a measure of Earth's pull on an object.		

Directions: Think about the things you have studied in this chapter. Then finish the sentence.

⓫ I am interested in learning more about _____

_____

_____

_____

Name _____ Date _____

Chapter 3

Chapter Test: How Do Forces Act?

Directions: Read each question. Then choose the correct answer.

1 Which of these is an example of a pull?

Ⓐ A baseball player throws a ball.

Ⓑ One magnet repels another magnet.

Ⓒ An apple falls from a tree to the ground.

Ⓓ A soccer player kicks the ball toward the goal.

2 Juan lets a ball go at the top of a ramp. What causes the ball to start moving down the ramp?

Ⓐ the size of the ball

Ⓑ the length of the ramp

Ⓒ the smooth surface of the ramp

Ⓓ the force of gravity acting on the ball

3 Rose and Gloria are pushing a ball as shown below.

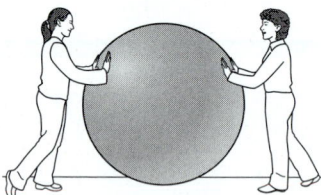

Why is the ball **not** moving?

Ⓐ They are both pushing the ball in the same direction.

Ⓑ They are both pushing the ball in different directions.

Ⓒ They are both pushing the ball with unequal forces.

Ⓓ They are both pushing the ball with equal forces.

GO ON

106

Grade 4 Physical Science

Name _____ Date _____   **Chapter 3**

Chapter Test — How Do Forces Act?

4 Ken and Steve pull as hard as they can on either end of a rope. What makes the rope slowly move toward Ken?

Ⓐ Ken is using more force than Steve to pull the rope.

Ⓑ Ken is moving in the opposite direction from Steve.

Ⓒ Ken's end of the rope has more mass than Steve's end.

Ⓓ Ken's end of the rope has less friction than Steve's end.

5 Martin pushes a 100g ball and a 500g ball from the same starting point with the same force. What will **most likely** happen?

Ⓐ The 500g ball will move more easily.

Ⓑ The 100g ball will move more easily

Ⓒ Both balls will travel at the same speed.

Ⓓ Both balls will travel in opposite directions.

6 Betty and Carlos are playing tennis. Betty hits the ball to Carlos. What will happen when Carlos hits the ball with his racket?

Ⓐ The force of friction pushing on the ball will increase.

Ⓑ The force of gravity pulling on the ball will increase.

Ⓒ The motion of the ball will stay the same.

Ⓓ The direction of the ball will change.

7 Julie is pushing Alan around on a merry-go-round. What can Julie do to make Alan go faster?

Ⓐ push with more force

Ⓑ pull instead of push

Ⓒ add the force of gravity to the merry-go-round

Ⓓ increase the friction of the merry-go-round

8 Two balls roll down a ramp. The first ball turns to the left, and the second ball rolls in a straight line. Which statement is true?

Ⓐ The motion of the balls is different.

Ⓑ The force of gravity on the balls is different.

Ⓒ The first ball has friction, but the second ball does not.

Ⓓ The first ball follows a pattern, but the second ball does not.

9 Susan wants to know a race car's speed. She knows the distance the car travels on the track. What else does Susan need to know to figure out the race car's speed?

Ⓐ the force of gravity on the race car

Ⓑ the mass of the race car

Ⓒ the time it takes to complete the race

Ⓓ the amount of friction on the racetrack

GO ON

Name _____ Date _____ Chapter 3

Chapter Test How Do Forces Act?

10 Dave rolls a toy car on a tile floor and on a carpet. What causes the car to roll more slowly on the carpet?

Ⓐ There is less friction on the carpet.

Ⓑ There is more friction on the carpet.

Ⓒ The force of gravity is weaker on the carpet.

Ⓓ The force of gravity is stronger on the carpet.

11 Brandon threw a ball straight up in the air. What made the ball change direction and come back down?

Ⓐ the speed of the ball

Ⓑ the force of the throw

Ⓒ push of air on the ball

Ⓓ the pull of gravity on the ball

Directions: Read the question. Then write your answer on the lines.

12 What is the scientific way to describe the weight of an object?

_____

_____

Test Score

_____ /13

Name _____ Date _____ **Chapter 4**

Chapter Self-Assessment — What Is Magnetism?

Directions: Write a ✓ in the box to show the answer that is true for you.

	Yes	Not Yet
❶ I can identify magnets.		
❷ I know how magnets function in everyday life.		
❸ I know that magnets can attract magnetic materials.		
❹ I know that magnets can attract and repel other magnets.		
❺ I can separate magnetic from non-magnetic materials.		
❻ I can describe the effects of a magnetic field.		
❼ I know that the force of magnetism decreases as distance from the magnet increases.		

Directions: Think about the things you have studied in this chapter. Then finish the sentence.

❽ I am interested in learning more about _____

_____

_____

_____

Name _____ Date _____ Chapter 4

Chapter Test — What Is Magnetism?

Directions: Read each question. Then choose the correct answer.

1 Mark places one magnet close to another magnet. When he does this, the magnets move toward each other. How can Mark explain this?

Ⓐ The magnetic field of one magnet is stronger than the other.

Ⓑ The north and south poles of the two magnets attract each other.

Ⓒ The magnetic fields of the magnets are too weak to repel each other.

Ⓓ The south pole of one magnet pulls on the south pole of the other magnet.

2 Which is an example of a magnet at work?

Ⓐ A compass points toward north.

Ⓑ A tack holds a calendar on a wall.

Ⓒ A nickel drops when put into a vending machine.

Ⓓ A horseshoe holds down paper on a wooden desk.

3 John has a copper penny, an iron nail, a plastic spoon, and an aluminum can. Which of John's objects are magnetic?

Ⓐ only the iron nail

Ⓑ only the aluminum can

Ⓒ the copper penny and the iron nail

Ⓓ the aluminum can and the plastic spoon

GO ON

Name _____ Date _____ **Chapter 4**

Chapter Test What Is Magnetism?

4 Tammy places iron filings in a magnet's magnetic field. What will **most likely** happen?

Ⓐ All of the iron filings will stay where Tammy placed them.

Ⓑ The magnet pulls the most distant iron filings toward itself.

Ⓒ The middle of the magnet will repel some of the iron filings.

Ⓓ Most of the iron filings will be pulled toward the magnet's poles.

5 Lisa placed two magnets 4 cm apart. The poles repelled and the magnets pushed away from each other. When the magnets were placed 8 cm apart, they did not move.

What happened as the distance between the magnets increased?

Ⓐ The magnetic poles reversed.

Ⓑ The force of magnetism decreased.

Ⓒ The magnets were no longer magnetic.

Ⓓ The magnetic force changed to attraction.

Directions: Read the question. Then write your answer on the lines.

6 Ken is doing an experiment on magnetism. He observes that a piece of paper is not pulled toward a magnet. He also observes that a paper clip is attracted to the magnet.

Explain Ken's results for both objects.

_____

_____

Test Score

_____ /7

Name _____ Date _____ Chapter 5

Chapter Self-Assessment — **What Are Some Forms of Energy?**

Directions: Write a ✓ in the box to show the answer that is true for you.

	Yes	Not Yet
❶ I know that motion is the result of energy being used.		
❷ I know that energy makes things move or change.		
❸ I can describe heat as the flow of energy from a warmer object to a cooler object.		
❹ I know that heat flows between objects until they are both the same temperature.		
❺ I know that heat is the energy produced when substances burn or when materials rub against each other.		
❻ I can identify materials that conduct heat well or poorly.		
❼ I know that light is a form of energy.		
❽ I know that light can be reflected from some objects.		
❾ I know that light can pass through some objects.		
❿ I know what chemical energy is.		

Directions: Think about the things you have studied in this chapter. Then finish the sentence.

⓫ I am interested in learning more about _____

_____

_____

_____

Name _____ Date _____   **Chapter 5**

Chapter Test | **What Are Some Forms of Energy?**

Directions: Read each question. Then choose the correct answer.

1 John poured hot chocolate into a cold mug. Why did the outside of the mug start to feel warm?

Ⓐ The mug lost heat energy to the hot chocolate.

Ⓑ The hot chocolate traded heat energy with the cold mug.

Ⓒ The heat energy from the hot chocolate flowed to the cold mug.

Ⓓ The heat energy in the mug and the hot chocolate was the same.

2 Dorothy lets go of a ball at the top of a hill. What kind of energy does the ball use as it moves down the hill?

Ⓐ mechanical energy

Ⓑ chemical energy

Ⓒ stored energy

Ⓓ heat energy

3 Which of these **best** describes the scientific idea of energy?

Ⓐ a force that can cause motion

Ⓑ the power to get a lot of work done

Ⓒ a source of fuel for our cars and homes

Ⓓ the ability to cause motion or create change

GO ON

Name _____ Date _____

Chapter 5

Chapter Test — **What Are Some Forms of Energy?**

4 Wayne put a cold brick on top of a hot brick. Which of these **best** describes what will happen to the bricks?

  Ⓐ The cold from the cold brick will flow to the hot brick.

  Ⓑ The heat from the hot brick will flow to the cold brick.

  Ⓒ Both bricks will get colder as time passes.

  Ⓓ Both bricks will get hotter as time passes.

5 Roy rubs a piece of sandpaper on a wooden bench and notices that the wood feels warm. Why does the rubbed wood become warm?

  Ⓐ Wood is a good conductor of heat.

  Ⓑ The rubbed wood absorbs heat from the air.

  Ⓒ Heat is produced as the sandpaper and the wood rub against each other.

  Ⓓ The heat from Roy's hand is transferred to the wood through the sandpaper.

6 Why are leather and plastic used to make safety clothing for people who work with heat?

  Ⓐ They can reflect light energy.

  Ⓑ They can absorb heat energy.

  Ⓒ They keep the workers cool.

  Ⓓ They are poor conductors of heat.

7 Campers use many different forms of energy when they go on a trip. Which of these is an example of the campers using light energy?

  Ⓐ rowing a boat to go fishing

  Ⓑ using a lantern to see at night

  Ⓒ pulling a rope to set up the tent

  Ⓓ burning sticks to heat up their food

GO ON

Grade 4 Physical Science

Name _____ Date _____

Chapter 5

Chapter Test **What Are Some Forms of Energy?**

8 Which of these is an example of chemical energy?

  Ⓐ wind turning a windmill

  Ⓑ a ball rolling down a hill

  Ⓒ gas burning to heat water

  Ⓓ water freezing to become ice

Directions: Read the question. Then write your answer on the lines.

9 Name one material that reflects light: _____

How does the material reflect the light?

_____

_____

Name one material that does **not** reflect light: _____

If light is not reflected, what happens when it shines on this material?

_____

_____

Test Score

_____ /10

115

Grade 4 Physical Science

Name _____ Date _____ **Chapter 6**

Chapter Self-Assessment — What Is Sound?

Directions: Write a ✓ in the box to show the answer that is true for you.

	Yes	Not Yet
❶ I know that energy exists in many forms.		
❷ I know that sound is a form of energy.		
❸ I know that vibrating objects make sound.		
❹ I know that sound can make things vibrate.		
❺ I can explain the relationship between vibrations and the volume of sound.		
❻ I know that faster vibrations mean higher pitch.		

Directions: Think about the things you have studied in this chapter. Then finish the sentence.

❼ I am interested in learning more about _____

_____

_____

_____

Name _____ Date _____ Chapter 6

Chapter Test — What Is Sound?

Directions: Read each question. Then choose the correct answer.

1 What causes sound energy when a person speaks?
- Ⓐ moving the lips
- Ⓑ breathing in air
- Ⓒ moving the tongue
- Ⓓ vibrating vocal cords

2 Which of these is true about sound?
- Ⓐ Sound is a form of energy.
- Ⓑ Sound waves can be seen.
- Ⓒ Sound is heard only by people.
- Ⓓ Sound can travel only through air.

3 Sarah is playing the guitar. How can she increase the volume of her playing?
- Ⓐ play the guitar quickly to create faster vibrations
- Ⓑ pluck the thinner strings to make smaller vibrations
- Ⓒ pluck the strings with more force to make larger vibrations
- Ⓓ play the guitar slowly so the strings can finish their vibrations

Name _____ Date _____ Chapter 6

Chapter Test: What Is Sound?

Directions: Read the question. Then write your answer on the lines.

4 Look at the musical instruments.

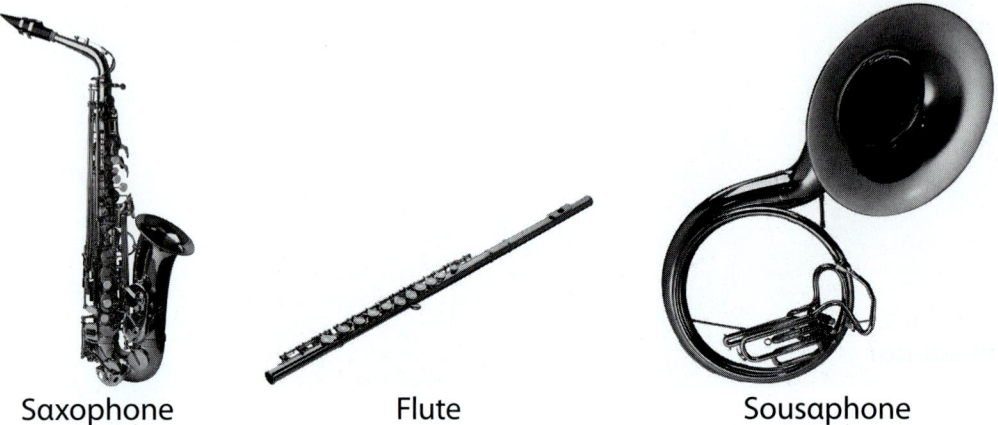

Saxophone   Flute   Sousaphone

The flute plays the highest notes, while the sousaphone can play the lowest. Which instrument makes sounds with the fastest vibrations?

_____

_____

Explain how the speed of the vibrations affects pitch.

_____

_____

Test Score ____/5

Name _____ Date _____ **Chapter 7**

Chapter Self-Assessment — What Is Electricity?

Directions: Write a ✓ in the box to show the answer that is true for you.

	Yes	Not Yet
❶ I know that electric circuits may produce light, heat, sound, and magnetic energy.		
❷ I can explain how static electricity affects the motion of objects.		
❸ I can describe how electrical energy is transferred and changed in a simple circuit.		
❹ I can identify objects as good conductors or poor conductors of electricity		
❺ I know that a simple circuit must be closed to conduct electricity.		
❻ I know that magnets and electricity produce forces.		
❼ I know that electric charges flowing through a wire can make an object work like a magnet.		
❽ I can compare simple and parallel circuits.		

Directions: Think about the things you have studied in this chapter. Then finish the sentence.

❾ I am interested in learning more about _____

_____

_____

_____

Name _____ Date _____

Chapter 7

Chapter Test What Is Electricity?

Directions: Read each question. Then choose the correct answer.

1 A circuit has a switch, a wire, a battery, and a bulb. When the switch is flipped, the light turns on. Which energy is used in this circuit when it is closed?

Ⓐ light

Ⓑ heat

Ⓒ sound

Ⓓ electrical

2 Jenny rubbed an air-filled balloon on her hair. She then touched the balloon to a wall and the balloon stuck to it. What made the balloon stick to the wall?

Ⓐ increased gravity

Ⓑ current electricity

Ⓒ static electricity

Ⓓ magnetic force

3 Four light bulbs are connected in a series circuit. What will happen if bulb 3 burns out?

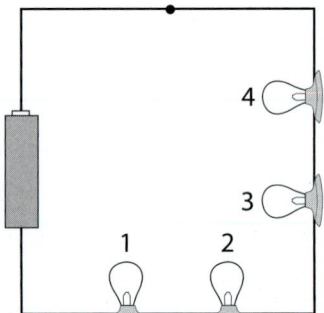

Ⓐ Only bulb 4 will be lit.

Ⓑ Bulbs 1, 2, and 4 will be lit.

Ⓒ Bulbs 1, 2, 3, and 4 will not light up.

Ⓓ Bulbs 1 and 2 will be lit, and 3 and 4 will not light up.

GO ON

Name _____ Date _____

Chapter 7

> **Chapter Test** What Is Electricity?

4 Which material would make the best conductor of electricity?

Ⓐ glass

Ⓑ copper

Ⓒ rubber

Ⓓ plastic

5 What is **most likely** the reason the light bulb in this circuit does not light up?

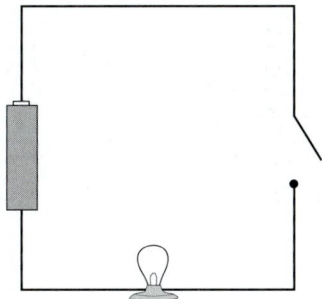

Ⓐ The circuit is open.

Ⓑ The circuit is simple.

Ⓒ The circuit is parallel.

Ⓓ The circuit needs more power.

6 How is a series circuit different from a parallel circuit?

Ⓐ A series circuit uses an electromagnet; a parallel circuit does not.

Ⓑ A series circuit uses current electricity; a parallel circuit uses static electricity.

Ⓒ In a series circuit, the electricity flows in one path; in a parallel circuit, the electricity can follow more than one path.

Ⓓ In a series circuit, if one light burns out, the others stay lit; in a parallel circuit, if one light burns out, the others burn out too.

GO ON

121   Grade 4 Physical Science

Chapter Test: What Is Electricity?

Chapter 7

7 Which of these describes electromagnets?

Ⓐ Electromagnets use magnets to make electricity.

Ⓑ Electromagnets produce static electricity.

Ⓒ Electromagnets use electricity to make a magnetic field.

Ⓓ Electromagnets are made using insulators of electricity.

Directions: Read the question. Then write your answer on the lines.

8 Adam makes an electromagnet and puts some metal paper clips near it.

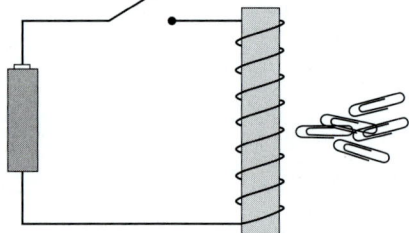

What will happen when he closes the circuit?

_____

_____

What will happen if he opens the circuit again?

_____

_____

_____

Test Score _____ /9

Physical Science Benchmark Test

Physical Science Benchmark Test.................................124

Benchmark Test

Purpose and Description

A Benchmark Test is available for the Physical Science Unit. The Benchmark Test uses multiple-choice and short constructed-response items to measure student understanding of the Physical Science concepts taught in this unit.

Administering the Test

Administer the Benchmark Test after evaluating the results of all the Chapter Tests and presenting any additional instruction if needed. Allow about 30 minutes for administration. Make a copy of the test for each student.

All directions may be read to the students. All test items, including any charts and diagrams, may be read to students if deemed necessary. Use a copy of the test to point out directions, test items, and response areas.

Introduce the test by telling students the purpose of the test.

- To begin the test, read the directions.
- Tell students how they are expected to respond to that type of item, for example, by filling in a circle.
- Give students time to work individually on the test, and allow a reasonable amount of time for them to complete it.
- Look to see that students are responding to the items in the correct manner.
- Read the directions and items in the test as necessary, explaining to students how they are expected to respond to any new item formats.

Students may not use their books during the test.

Scoring the Tests and Using the Results

Score the Benchmark Test with the Answer Key on page 178. Use the Student Profile on page 179 to determine if students need additional instruction in any of the science concepts presented. For more information on scoring, see page 133.

Name _____ Date _____

Benchmark Test · Physical Science

Directions: Read each question. Then choose the correct answer.

1 Which of these is magnetic?
- Ⓐ a plastic ruler
- Ⓑ a glass marble
- Ⓒ a copper penny
- Ⓓ a nickel necklace

2 What are humans, buildings, oceans, and plants all made of?
- Ⓐ air
- Ⓑ water
- Ⓒ matter
- Ⓓ carbon

3 What does **all** matter have?
- Ⓐ air
- Ⓑ heat
- Ⓒ mass
- Ⓓ water

Name _____ Date _____

Benchmark Test — Physical Science

4 Adam wants to compare two materials that look very similar. How can he better observe the parts that make up each material?

Ⓐ He can wash the materials in water.

Ⓑ He can mix the two materials together.

Ⓒ He can hold the materials closer to his eyes.

Ⓓ He can look at the materials through a hand lens.

5 Stephanie put two substances into a bowl. The substances are unevenly spread out. Each substance kept its original properties and could easily be separated. What is true about the material in the bowl?

Ⓐ The two substances formed a solution.

Ⓑ The two substances formed a mixture.

Ⓒ The two substances have different masses.

Ⓓ The two substances have the same properties.

6 Tammy wants to measure the volume of a cardboard box. Which tool could she use?

Ⓐ a ruler

Ⓑ a balance

Ⓒ a spring scale

Ⓓ a graduated cylinder

GO ON

Benchmark Test: Physical Science

7 How can a material be changed from the solid state to the liquid state?

  Ⓐ Heat the material.

  Ⓑ Shake the material.

  Ⓒ Freeze the material.

  Ⓓ Break the material into smaller pieces.

8 Kathy combines flour, water, and yeast to make bread dough. Which of these properties **most likely** stays the same when the dough becomes bread?

  Ⓐ texture

  Ⓑ shape

  Ⓒ color

  Ⓓ size

9 A ball was lying still on flat ground, and then it started rolling. What caused the ball to start rolling?

  Ⓐ Force was applied to the ball.

  Ⓑ Gravity pulled the ball forward.

  Ⓒ The mass of the ball increased.

  Ⓓ Friction on the ball was removed.

Name _____ Date _____

Benchmark Test — Physical Science

10 Harold was able to push a small toy car, but when he tried to push a car with a greater mass, he could not move it. What does he need?

Ⓐ more force

Ⓑ less gravity

Ⓒ more friction

Ⓓ less speed

11 Kelly is pushing Victor on a swing. Victor asks to be pushed harder. What will happen if Kelly pushes the swing harder?

Ⓐ The swing will go slower.

Ⓑ The swing will go higher.

Ⓒ The swing will stop soon.

Ⓓ The swing will change direction.

12 Shawn uses a trampoline to jump high into the air. What makes him come back down to the surface of the trampoline?

Ⓐ air

Ⓑ a push

Ⓒ gravity

Ⓓ friction

GO ON

Name _____ Date _____

Benchmark Test — Physical Science

13 Which of these objects uses a magnet to work?

  Ⓐ a nail

  Ⓑ a compass

  Ⓒ a paper clip

  Ⓓ a water faucet

14 Julia hits a drum with a drumstick and makes it vibrate. Then she rests her hand on the drum. What happens to the sound of the drum?

  Ⓐ The sound stops because the vibrations have stopped.

  Ⓑ The sound stops because it cannot go around her hand.

  Ⓒ The sound becomes clearer because the vibrations have stopped.

  Ⓓ The sound decreases in pitch because the vibrations have slowed down.

15 Annie pours hot water into a cool cup. Soon the cup becomes hot. Why does the cup become hot?

  Ⓐ The cup is a good insulator.

  Ⓑ Annie's hands warmed the cup.

  Ⓒ The cup absorbed heat from the air.

  Ⓓ The heat from the water flowed to the cup.

GO ON

Name _____ Date _____

Benchmark Test — Physical Science

16 When the electricity goes out, Nicole lights some candles. What kind of energy are the candles producing?

Ⓐ light energy

Ⓑ sound energy

Ⓒ stored energy

Ⓓ electrical energy

17 What happens when the vibrations of a drum get larger?

Ⓐ The pitch increases.

Ⓑ The pitch decreases.

Ⓒ The volume increases.

Ⓓ The volume decreases.

18 An electric circuit in a machine made music play. What type of energy did the circuit **mostly** produce?

Ⓐ heat

Ⓑ light

Ⓒ sound

Ⓓ magnetic

19 How does pushing on a doorbell produce a sound?

Ⓐ The force of the push sends electrical charges through the air.

Ⓑ The force of the push is transformed into sound vibrations in the air.

Ⓒ Electricity takes the quiet sound of the push and makes it much louder.

Ⓓ A circuit is closed, causing an electromagnet to make a hammer hit a bell.

GO ON

Name _____ Date _____

Benchmark Test Physical Science

20 Jason plucks two strings on a guitar. The second string has a higher pitch than the first string. What causes the difference in pitch?

Ⓐ The second string is longer.

Ⓑ The second string vibrates faster.

Ⓒ The first string was plucked harder.

Ⓓ The first string has a lower volume.

21 Christopher coiled a wire around a nail and connected the wire to a battery and a switch in an electric circuit. When he closed the circuit, paper clips lying nearby stuck to the nail. What has **most likely** happened?

Ⓐ Electricity changed direction when the circuit was closed.

Ⓑ The closed circuit created static electricity in the paper clips.

Ⓒ The paper clips became insulators when the circuit was closed.

Ⓓ Electric charges flowed through the wire and made the nail magnetic.

Directions: Read each question. Then write your answers on the lines.

22 How do scientists define energy?

_____

Write one example of energy, and explain how it fits the scientific definition of energy.

_____

_____

GO ON

Benchmark Test Physical Science

23. Look at the pictures of Circuit 1 and Circuit 2. Write the name of the type of each circuit.

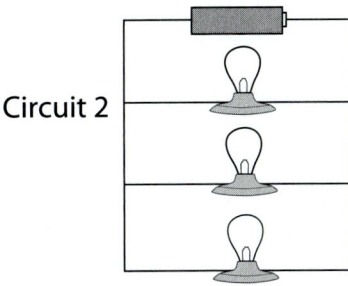

Circuit 1

Circuit 2

Type: _____ Type: _____

What will happen if a bulb goes out in Circuit 1?

_____

What will happen if a bulb goes out in Circuit 2?

_____

Test Score

_____ /25

Scoring and Reporting Tools

Life Science Student Profiles, Answer Keys, and Class Profile 134
Earth Science Student Profiles, Answer Keys, and Class Profile 149
Physical Science Student Profiles, Answer Keys, and Class Profile 164

Student Profiles and Answer Keys

Teachers can score the students' tests and report their results by hand using the Student Profiles and Answer Keys. These pages include the correct responses to multiple-choice items as well as item-specific rubrics for the short constructed-response items in each Chapter Test and the Benchmark Test. Make copies of each Student Profile and Answer Key for every student.

Class Profile

Use the Class Profile to record the Chapter Test and Benchmark Test scores for all the students in your class.

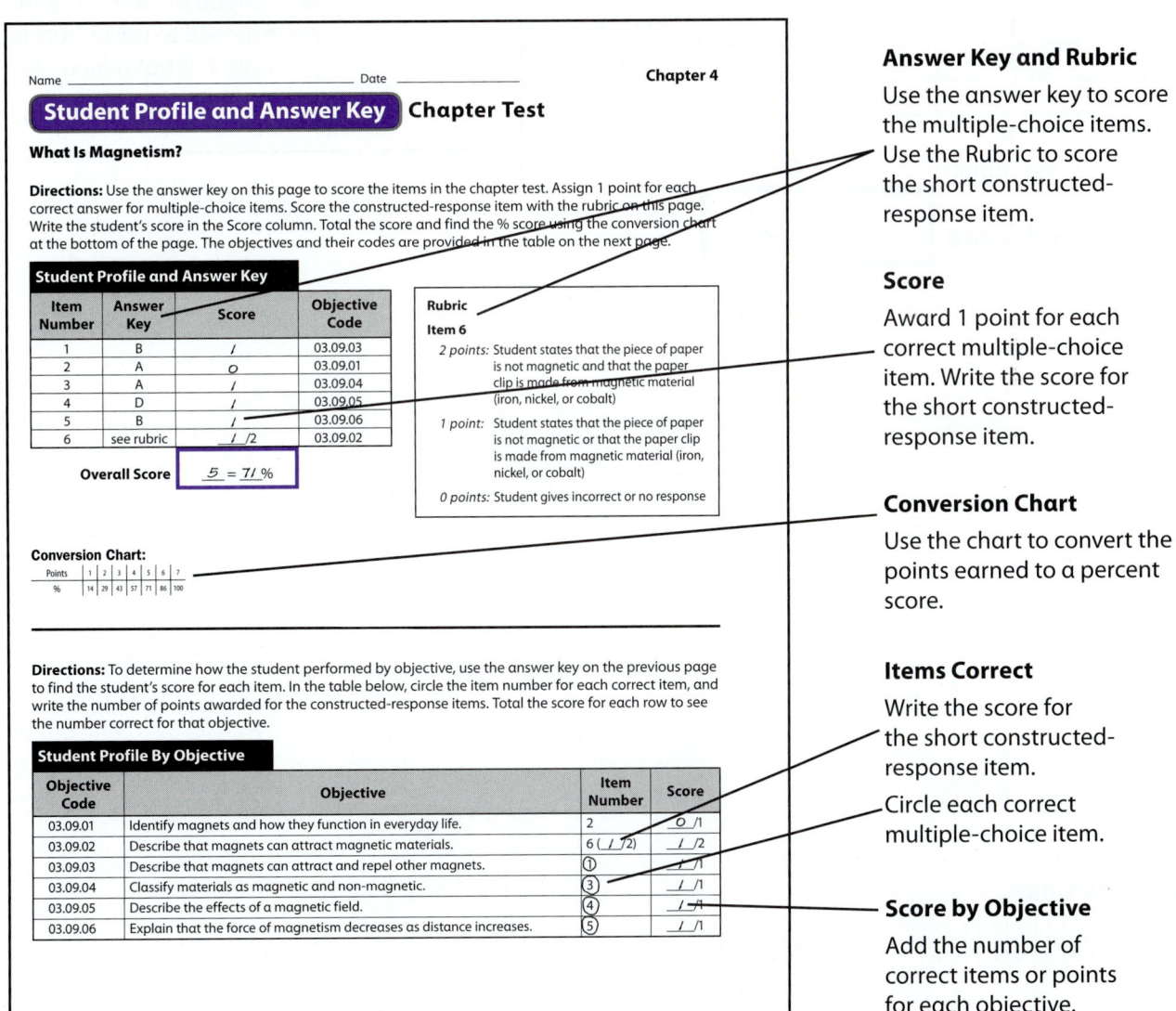

Answer Key and Rubric

Use the answer key to score the multiple-choice items. Use the Rubric to score the short constructed-response item.

Score

Award 1 point for each correct multiple-choice item. Write the score for the short constructed-response item.

Conversion Chart

Use the chart to convert the points earned to a percent score.

Items Correct

Write the score for the short constructed-response item.

Circle each correct multiple-choice item.

Score by Objective

Add the number of correct items or points for each objective.

Name _____ Date _____ Chapter 1

Student Profile and Answer Key — Chapter Test

How Do Plants Grow and Reproduce?

Directions: Use the answer key on this page to score the items in the chapter test. Assign 1 point for each correct answer for multiple-choice items. Score the constructed-response item with the rubric on this page. Write the student's score in the Score column. Total the score and find the % score using the conversion chart at the bottom of the page. The objectives and their codes are provided in the table on the next page.

Student Profile and Answer Key

Item Number	Answer Key	Score	Objective Code
1	D		01.06.10
2	A		01.06.01
3	C		01.06.02
4	B		01.06.03
5	D		01.06.04
6	B		01.06.05
7	D		01.06.09
8	A		01.06.07
9	C		01.06.11
10	B		01.06.06
11	see rubric	___/2	01.06.08
Overall Score		___ = ___%	

Rubric

Item 11

2 points: Student writes pollination and fertilization and states that the tree is not exposed to pollinators indoors, so these processes are not taking place

1 point: Student writes pollination and fertilization or states that the tree is not exposed to pollinators indoors, so pollination is not taking place

0 points: Student gives incorrect or no response

Conversion Chart:

Points	1	2	3	4	5	6	7	8	9	10	11	12
%	8	17	25	33	42	50	58	67	75	83	92	100

Name _____ Date _____ **Chapter 1**

Student Profile and Answer Key — Chapter Test continued

How Do Plants Grow and Reproduce?

Directions: To determine how the student performed by objective, use the answer key on the previous page to find the student's score for each item. In the table below, circle the item number for each correct item, and write the number of points awarded for the constructed-response items. Total the score for each row to see the number correct for that objective.

Student Profile By Objective

Objective Code	Objective	Item Number	Score
01.06.01	Identify the major structures of a seed plant and relate them to their functions.	2	___/1
01.06.02	Classify plants according to their characteristics.	3	___/1
01.06.03	Describe the main processes involved in the reproduction of flowering plants.	4	___/1
01.06.04	Compare and contrast the life cycles of flowering plants and conifers.	5	___/1
01.06.05	Identify individual differences in organisms of the same kind.	6	___/1
01.06.06	Explain that although most characteristics of plants are inherited, some characteristics can be affected by factors in a plant's environment.	10	___/1
01.06.07	Compare the main reproductive structures of flowering plants and conifers.	8	___/1
01.06.08	Describe the processes of pollination and fertilization in flowering plants.	11 (___/2)	___/2
01.06.09	Describe the main processes of seed and fruit formation in flowering plants.	7	___/1
01.06.10	Describe how the seeds of flowering plants are dispersed.	1	___/1
01.06.11	Describe the germination and growth of flowering plants.	9	___/1

Name _____ Date _____ Chapter 2

Student Profile and Answer Key — Chapter Test

How Do Animals Grow and Change?

Directions: Use the answer key on this page to score the items in the chapter test. Assign 1 point for each correct answer for multiple-choice items. Score the constructed-response item with the rubric on this page. Write the student's score in the Score column. Total the score and find the % score using the conversion chart at the bottom of the page. The objectives and their codes are provided in the table on the next page.

Student Profile and Answer Key

Item Number	Answer Key	Score	Objective Code
1	D		01.07.01
2	C		01.07.02
3	A		01.07.03
4	D		01.07.04
5	A		01.07.05
6	D		01.07.06
7	D		01.07.07
8	see rubric	___/2	01.07.08

Overall Score ___ = ___%

Rubric

Item 8

2 points: Student states that it is a learned behavior and states that the rat had to become familiar with the maze by practicing, and student states that a wild rat could also learn the maze through practice or that it could not get through the maze on the first try because it had not learned how

1 point: Student states that it is a learned behavior and states that the rat had to become familiar with the maze by practicing, or student states that a wild rat could also learn the maze through practice or that it could not get through the maze on the first try because it had not learned how

0 points: Student gives incorrect or no response

Conversion Chart:

Points	1	2	3	4	5	6	7	8	9
%	11	22	33	44	56	67	78	89	100

Name _____ Date _____ Chapter 2

Student Profile and Answer Key | Chapter Test continued

How Do Animals Grow and Change?

Directions: To determine how the student performed by objective, use the answer key on the previous page to find the student's score for each item. In the table below, circle the item number for each correct item, and write the number of points awarded for the constructed-response items. Total the score for each row to see the number correct for that objective.

Student Profile By Objective

Objective Code	Objective	Item Number	Score
01.07.01	Describe the different life cycles of animals and identify the different stages of these life cycles.	1	___/1
01.07.02	Recognize that living things grow and change and need water, nutrients, and air to survive.	2	___/1
01.07.03	Compare and contrast the similarities and differences among offspring of different animal life cycles.	3	___/1
01.07.04	Describe the process of molting during the life cycles of incomplete metamorphosis.	4	___/1
01.07.05	Observe that traits of animals are inherited from their parents and that individuals vary within every species.	5	___/1
01.07.06	Describe animal behaviors that result from heredity.	6	___/1
01.07.07	Recognize that acquired traits in animals can result from the environment.	7	___/1
01.07.08	Describe animal behaviors that result from learning.	8 (___/2)	___/2

Name _____ Date _____   Chapter 3

Student Profile and Answer Key — Chapter Test

How Do Plants and Animals Depend on Their Environment?

Directions: Use the answer key on this page to score the items in the chapter test. Assign 1 point for each correct answer for multiple-choice items. Score the constructed-response item with the rubric on this page. Write the student's score in the Score column. Total the score and find the % score using the conversion chart at the bottom of the page. The objectives and their codes are provided in the table on the next page.

Student Profile and Answer Key

Item Number	Answer Key	Score	Objective Code
1	A		01.08.01
2	C		01.08.02
3	C		01.08.03
4	B		01.08.04
5	A		01.08.05
6	C		01.08.06
7	D		01.08.07
8	B		01.08.08
9	A		01.08.12
10	D		01.08.09
11	B		01.08.10
12	A		01.08.16
13	D		01.08.17
14	B		01.08.19
15	D		01.08.11
16	A		01.08.15
17	C		01.08.13
18	B		01.08.14
19	see rubric	___/2	01.08.18

Overall Score ___ = ___%

Rubric

Item 19

2 points: Student provides two things trees might compete over, such as nutrients from the soil, space, sunlight, or water

1 point: Student provides one thing trees might compete over

0 points: Student gives incorrect or no response

Conversion Chart:

Points	1	2	3	4	5	6	7	8	9	10	11	12	13	14	15	16	17	18	19	20
%	5	10	15	20	25	30	35	40	45	50	55	60	65	70	75	80	85	90	95	100

Name _____ Date _____ **Chapter 3**

Student Profile and Answer Key — **Chapter Test** continued

How Do Plants and Animals Depend on Their Environment?

Directions: To determine how the student performed by objective, use the answer key on the previous page to find the student's score for each item. In the table below, circle the item number for each correct item, and write the number of points awarded for the constructed-response items. Total the score for each row to see the number correct for that objective.

Student Profile By Objective

Objective Code	Objective	Item Number	Score
01.08.01	Identify the needs of living things.	1	___/1
01.08.02	Recognize communities as groups of living things that depend on each other for food.	2	___/1
01.08.03	Recognize that green plants are producers because they make food using sunlight, water, and air.	3	___/1
01.08.04	Distinguish herbivores and carnivores.	4	___/1
01.08.05	Identify examples of consumers as either herbivores or carnivores.	5	___/1
01.08.06	Describe omnivores.	6	___/1
01.08.07	Identify examples of consumers that are omnivores.	7	___/1
01.08.08	Describe the role of decomposers in a community.	8	___/1
01.08.09	Describe how energy passes from one living thing to another in a community.	10	___/1
01.08.10	Recognize that several interacting food chains form a food web.	11	___/1
01.08.11	Identify the role that each organism in a food web plays.	15	___/1
01.08.12	Describe ways that organisms interact with one another.	9	___/1
01.08.13	Classify living things as predators or prey.	17	___/1
01.08.14	Explain how predators and prey depend on each other.	18	___/1
01.08.15	Explain how parasites get their food.	16	___/1
01.08.16	Recognize examples of parasites and their hosts.	12	___/1
01.08.17	Describe examples of how plants and animals interact with one another.	13	___/1
01.08.18	Explain how individuals within a species may compete with each other.	19 (___/2)	___/2
01.08.19	Identify the kinds of resources for which living things compete.	14	___/1

Name _____ Date _____ Chapter 4

Student Profile and Answer Key — Chapter Test

How Do Adaptations Help Living Things Survive?

Directions: Use the answer key on this page to score the items in the chapter test. Assign 1 point for each correct answer for multiple-choice items. Score the constructed-response item with the rubric on this page. Write the student's score in the Score column. Total the score and find the % score using the conversion chart at the bottom of the page. The objectives and their codes are provided in the table on the next page.

Student Profile and Answer Key

Item Number	Answer Key	Score	Objective Code
1	C		01.09.10
2	D		01.09.14
3	C		01.09.01
4	A		01.09.04
5	A		01.09.06
6	D		01.09.07
7	B		01.09.08
8	C		01.09.09
9	B		01.09.03
10	C		01.09.11
11	D		01.09.12
12	D		01.09.13
13	B		01.09.02
14	D		01.09.19
15	D		01.09.16
16	A		01.09.17
17	C		01.09.18
18	A		01.09.15
19	see rubric	___/2	01.09.05

Overall Score ___ = ___%

Rubric

Item 19

2 points: Student states that blending into its environment helps the chameleon avoid predators and gives an example of another adaptation that an animal can use to protect itself, such as having a shell or thick body covering or showing quills to scare off predators

1 point: Student states that blending into its environment helps the chameleon avoid predators or gives an example of another adaptation that an animal can use to protect itself

0 points: Student gives incorrect or no response

Conversion Chart:

Points	1	2	3	4	5	6	7	8	9	10	11	12	13	14	15	16	17	18	19	20
%	5	10	15	20	25	30	35	40	45	50	55	60	65	70	75	80	85	90	95	100

Name _____ Date _____ **Chapter 4**

Student Profile and Answer Key — **Chapter Test** continued

How Do Adaptations Help Living Things Survive?

Directions: To determine how the student performed by objective, use the answer key on the previous page to find the student's score for each item. In the table below, circle the item number for each correct item, and write the number of points awarded for the constructed-response items. Total the score for each row to see the number correct for that objective.

Student Profile By Objective

Objective Code	Objective	Item Number	Score
01.09.01	Explain how an adaptation can help a living thing survive.	3	___/1
01.09.02	Explain how adaptations for movement can help a living thing survive.	13	___/1
01.09.03	Recognize that hunger is an internal signal that causes an animal to hunt for food.	9	___/1
01.09.04	Explain how an animal uses its adaptations for getting food.	4	___/1
01.09.05	Explain how animals use an adaptation for defense and protection.	19 (___/2)	___/2
01.09.06	Distinguish between an adaptation and a variation.	5	___/1
01.09.07	Identify the importance of adaptations for sensing.	6	___/1
01.09.08	Explain advantages of animals using sound to communicate.	7	___/1
01.09.09	Identify examples of adaptations of animals for reproduction.	8	___/1
01.09.10	Identify adaptations of plants that reduce water loss.	1	___/1
01.09.11	Describe an adaptation that plants use for defense.	10	___/1
01.09.12	Explain how flowers are adaptations for plant reproduction.	11	___/1
01.09.13	Explain how seeds are adaptations for plant reproduction.	12	___/1
01.09.14	Explain how fruits are adaptations for plant reproduction.	2	___/1
01.09.15	Recognize fossils as the remains or traces of organisms that once lived.	18	___/1
01.09.16	Explain how scientists use fossils in the study of Earth's history.	15	___/1
01.09.17	Identify examples of modern plants that resemble a fossilized species.	16	___/1
01.09.18	Identify examples of modern animals that resemble a fossilized species.	17	___/1
01.09.19	Explain why some living things were able to survive for a long time while others became extinct.	14	___/1

Name _____ Date _____ Chapter 5

Student Profile and Answer Key — Chapter Test

How Do Living Things Interact with Their Environment?

Directions: Use the answer key on this page to score the items in the chapter test. Assign 1 point for each correct answer for multiple-choice items. Score the constructed-response item with the rubric on this page. Write the student's score in the Score column. Total the score and find the % score using the conversion chart at the bottom of the page. The objectives and their codes are provided in the table on the next page.

Student Profile and Answer Key

Item Number	Answer Key	Score	Objective Code
1	B		01.10.04
2	D		01.10.02
3	C		01.10.03
4	A		01.10.01
5	B		01.10.05
6	C		01.10.06
7	C		01.10.07
8	D		01.10.08
9	C		01.10.09
10	D		01.10.11
11	see rubric	___/2	01.10.10

Overall Score ___ = ___%

Rubric

Item 11

- **2 points:** Student states one way that people affect their environment in a harmful way and provides a possible solution to the problem
- **1 point:** Student states one way that people affect their environment in a harmful way or provides a possible solution to an environmental problem
- **0 points:** Student gives incorrect or no response

Conversion Chart:

Points	1	2	3	4	5	6	7	8	9	10	11	12
%	8	17	25	33	42	50	58	67	75	83	92	100

Name _____ Date _____ Chapter 5

Student Profile and Answer Key — Chapter Test continued

How Do Living Things Interact with Their Environment?

Directions: To determine how the student performed by objective, use the answer key on the previous page to find the student's score for each item. In the table below, circle the item number for each correct item, and write the number of points awarded for the constructed-response items. Total the score for each row to see the number correct for that objective.

Student Profile By Objective

Objective Code	Objective	Item Number	Score
01.10.01	Recognize ways that plants and animals can change the environment.	4	___/1
01.10.02	Give examples of how plants change based on the seasons.	2	___/1
01.10.03	Explain how plants adapt to the changing of the seasons in their environment.	3	___/1
01.10.04	Give some examples of how animals adapt to the changing of the seasons in their environment.	1	___/1
01.10.05	Explain how animals adapt to the changing of the seasons in their environment.	5	___/1
01.10.06	Explain how plants can change the environment in many ways.	6	___/1
01.10.07	Describe how plants and animals can harm an environment.	7	___/1
01.10.08	Explain how animals can change the environment by making homes and changing soil.	8	___/1
01.10.09	Explain how animals can change the environment by grazing and feeding.	9	___/1
01.10.10	Explain that humans can change the environment in beneficial or harmful ways.	11 (___/2)	___/2
01.10.11	Recognize that humans depend on their environments to meet their needs.	10	___/1

Name _____ Date _____ Chapter 6

Student Profile and Answer Key — Chapter Test

How Do the Parts of an Organism Work Together?

Directions: Use the answer key on this page to score the items in the chapter test. Assign 1 point for each correct answer for multiple-choice items. Score the constructed-response item with the rubric on this page. Write the student's score in the Score column. Total the score and find the % score using the conversion chart at the bottom of the page. The objectives and their codes are provided in the table on the next page.

Student Profile and Answer Key

Item Number	Answer Key	Score	Objective Code
1	B		01.11.01
2	D		01.11.02
3	A		01.11.03
4	C		01.11.05
5	A		01.11.06
6	B		01.11.04
7	C		01.11.08
8	C		01.11.09
9	A		01.11.10
10	see rubric	___/2	01.11.07

Overall Score ___ = ___%

Rubric

Item 10

- **2 points:** Student describes a voluntary/controlled action, such as moving an arm, and an involuntary/automatic action, such as the heart beating
- **1 point:** Student describes a voluntary/controlled action or an involuntary/automatic action
- **0 points:** Student gives incorrect or no response

Conversion Chart:

Points	1	2	3	4	5	6	7	8	9	10	11
%	9	18	27	36	45	55	64	73	82	91	100

Name _____ Date _____ **Chapter 6**

Student Profile and Answer Key — Chapter Test continued

How Do the Parts of an Organism Work Together?

Directions: To determine how the student performed by objective, use the answer key on the previous page to find the student's score for each item. In the table below, circle the item number for each correct item, and write the number of points awarded for the constructed-response items. Total the score for each row to see the number correct for that objective.

Student Profile By Objective

Objective Code	Objective	Item Number	Score
01.11.01	Explain that humans and other living things have different body parts that help them get what they need to survive.	1	___/1
01.11.02	Recognize that animals are composed of different parts performing different functions and working together for the well-being of the organism.	2	___/1
01.11.03	Describe the major organs of the circulatory system and how they function.	3	___/1
01.11.04	Describe the major organs of the respiratory system and how they function.	6	___/1
01.11.05	Describe the major organs of the digestive system and how they function.	4	___/1
01.11.06	Describe the major organs of the skeletal system and how they function.	5	___/1
01.11.07	Describe the major organs of the muscular system and how they function.	10 (___/2)	___/2
01.11.08	Describe the major organs of the nervous system and how they function.	7	___/1
01.11.09	Recognize that eating a balanced diet and getting regular exercise are good health habits.	8	___/1
01.11.10	Recognize that avoiding drugs, alcohol, and tobacco, as well as washing hands frequently are good health habits.	9	___/1

Name _____ Date _____ **Life Science**

Student Profile and Answer Key — Benchmark Test

Directions: Use the answer key on this page to score the items in the benchmark test. Assign 1 point for each correct answer for multiple-choice items. Score the constructed-response items with the rubrics on this page. Write the student's score in the Score column. Total the score and calculate the % score. The objectives and their codes are provided in a table on the next page.

Student Profile and Answer Key

Item Number	Answer Key	Score	Objective Code
1	B		01.08.03
2	A		01.06.03
3	D		01.06.04
4	D		01.06.10
5	D		01.07.01
6	A		01.07.05
7	A		01.07.07
8	D		01.08.02
9	C		01.06.02
10	C		01.08.09
11	B		01.08.14
12	C		01.08.18
13	D		01.09.01
14	D		01.09.03
15	A		01.09.16
16	B		01.10.01
17	D		01.10.03
18	B		01.10.05
19	C		01.10.10
20	D		01.11.02
21	B		01.11.09
22	see rubric	___/2	01.06.07
23	see rubric	___/2	01.07.03

Overall Score ___ × 4 = ___%

Rubric

Item 22

2 points: Student writes both a similarity and a difference between the reproductive structures of a rose bush and a pine tree, such as that they both have seeds, but a pine tree/conifer uses cones and a rose bush has flowers

1 point: Student writes either a similarity or a difference between the reproductive structures of a rose bush and a pine tree

0 points: Student gives incorrect or no response

Item 23

2 points: Student writes both a similarity (both start out as eggs) and a difference (when the offspring emerge from the eggs, sea turtles look like adults but butterflies are caterpillars, looking more like worms than adult butterflies) between baby sea turtles and butterflies

1 point: Student writes either a similarity or a difference between baby sea turtles and butterflies

0 points: Student gives incorrect or no response

Name _____ Date _____ **Life Science**

Student Profile and Answer Key — Benchmark Test continued

Directions: To determine how the student performed by objective, use the answer key on the previous page to find the student's score for each item. In the table below, circle the item number for each correct item, and write the number of points awarded for the constructed-response items. Total the score for each row to see the number correct for that objective.

Student Profile By Objective

Objective Code	Objective	Item Number	Score
01.06.02	Classify plants according to their characteristics.	9	___/1
01.06.03	Describe the main processes involved in the reproduction of flowering plants.	2	___/1
01.06.04	Compare and contrast the life cycles of flowering plants and conifers.	3	___/1
01.06.07	Compare the main reproductive structures of flowering plants and conifers.	22 (___/2)	___/2
01.06.10	Describe how the seeds of flowering plants are dispersed.	4	___/1
01.07.01	Describe the different life cycles of animals and identify the different stages of these life cycles.	5	___/1
01.07.03	Compare and contrast the similarities and differences among offspring of different animal life cycles.	23 (___/2)	___/2
01.07.05	Observe that traits of animals are inherited from their parents and that individuals vary within every species.	6	___/1
01.07.07	Recognize that acquired traits in animals can result from the environment.	7	___/1
01.08.02	Recognize communities as groups of living things that depend on each other for food.	8	___/1
01.08.03	Recognize that green plants are producers because they make food using sunlight, water, and air.	1	___/1
01.08.09	Describe how energy passes from one living thing to another in a community.	10	___/1
01.08.14	Explain how predators and prey depend on each other.	11	___/1
01.08.18	Explain how individuals within a species may compete with each other.	12	___/1
01.09.01	Explain how an adaptation can help a living thing survive.	13	___/1
01.09.03	Recognize that hunger is an internal signal that causes an animal to hunt for food.	14	___/1
01.09.16	Explain how scientists use fossils in the study of Earth's history.	15	___/1
01.10.01	Recognize ways that plants and animals can change the environment.	16	___/1
01.10.03	Explain how plants adapt to the changing of the seasons in their environment.	17	___/1
01.10.05	Explain how animals adapt to the changing of the seasons in their environment.	18	___/1
01.10.10	Explain that humans can change the environment in beneficial or harmful ways.	19	___/1
01.11.02	Recognize that animals are composed of different parts performing different functions and working together for the well-being of the organism.	20	___/1
01.11.09	Recognize that eating a balanced diet and getting regular exercise are good health habits.	21	___/1

Class Profile — Life Science

Directions: Write student names below. Record student Chapter Test and Benchmark Test scores in the columns to the right.

Student Name	Chapter Test 1	Chapter Test 2	Chapter Test 3	Chapter Test 4	Chapter Test 5	Chapter Test 6	Benchmark Test

Name _____ Date _____

Chapter 1

Student Profile and Answer Key — Chapter Test

How Do Earth and Its Moon Move?

Directions: Use the answer key on this page to score the items in the chapter test. Assign 1 point for each correct answer for multiple-choice items. Score the constructed-response item with the rubric on this page. Write the student's score in the Score column. Total the score and find the % score using the conversion chart at the bottom of the page. The objectives and their codes are provided in the table on the next page.

Student Profile and Answer Key

Item Number	Answer Key	Score	Objective Code
1	A		02.09.04
2	D		02.09.01
3	D		02.09.02
4	C		02.09.03
5	B		02.09.06
6	C		02.09.07
7	B		02.09.12
8	A		02.09.09
9	C		02.09.10
10	B		02.09.11
11	D		02.09.14
12	C		02.09.13
13	A		02.09.08
14	A		02.09.15
15	see rubric	___/2	02.09.05

Overall Score ___ = ___%

Rubric

Item 15

2 points: Student states that the moon will be west of where it was/the telephone pole farther away from the tall building because the moon seems to move from east to west or because Earth rotates on its axis

1 point: Student states that the moon will be west of where it was/the telephone pole farther away from the tall building or that the moon seems to move from east to west or that Earth rotates on its axis

0 points: Student gives incorrect or no response

Conversion Chart:

Points	1	2	3	4	5	6	7	8	9	10	11	12	13	14	15	16
%	6	13	19	25	31	38	44	50	56	63	69	75	81	88	94	100

Name _____ Date _____ Chapter 1

Student Profile and Answer Key — Chapter Test continued

How Do Earth and Its Moon Move?

Directions: To determine how the student performed by objective, use the answer key on the previous page to find the student's score for each item. In the table below, circle the item number for each correct item, and write the number of points awarded for the constructed-response items. Total the score for each row to see the number correct for that objective.

Student Profile By Objective

Objective Code	Objective	Item Number	Score
02.09.01	Identify the movements of Earth and the moon.	2	___/1
02.09.02	Compare and contrast the characteristics of the sun, moon, and Earth.	3	___/1
02.09.03	Explain that the spin of Earth creates day and night.	4	___/1
02.09.04	Describe the apparent movement of the sun across the sky.	1	___/1
02.09.05	Describe the apparent movement of the moon across the sky.	15 (___/2)	___/2
02.09.06	Explain that Earth is tilted on its axis.	5	___/1
02.09.07	Describe the orbit of Earth around the sun as it defines a year.	6	___/1
02.09.08	Explain that Earth's movement and position cause the seasons.	13	___/1
02.09.09	Explain that Earth's movement and position cause the seasons, including summer and fall.	8	___/1
02.09.10	Explain that Earth's movement and position cause the seasons, including winter and spring.	9	___/1
02.09.11	Identify the sun, other stars, and the moon as common objects in the sky.	10	___/1
02.09.12	Identify and observe the moon as a common object in the sky.	7	___/1
02.09.13	Identify the characteristics of the moon.	12	___/1
02.09.14	Describe the motion of the moon around Earth.	11	___/1
02.09.15	Explain how the visible shape of the moon follows a predictable cycle.	14	___/1

Name _____ Date _____

Chapter 2

Student Profile and Answer Key — Chapter Test

How Are Rocks Alike and Different?

Directions: Use the answer key on this page to score the items in the chapter test. Assign 1 point for each correct answer for multiple-choice items. Score the constructed-response item with the rubric on this page. Write the student's score in the Score column. Total the score and find the % score using the conversion chart at the bottom of the page. The objectives and their codes are provided in the table on the next page.

Student Profile and Answer Key

Item Number	Answer Key	Score	Objective Code
1	A		02.10.09
2	B		02.10.02
3	D		02.10.15
4	B		02.10.04
5	B		02.10.05
6	C		02.10.06
7	C		02.10.07
8	A		02.10.01
9	A		02.10.10
10	C		02.10.11
11	D		02.10.12
12	A		02.10.13
13	A		02.10.14
14	D		02.10.03
15	see rubric	___/2	02.10.08

Overall Score ___ = ___%

Rubric

Item 15

2 points: Student identifies a microscope or magnifying glass as an appropriate tool and states that the tool would be helpful for viewing details in the rock that are difficult to see with the eye alone

1 point: Student identifies a microscope or magnifying glass as an appropriate tool or states that the tool would be helpful for viewing details in the rock that are difficult to see with the eye alone

0 points: Student gives incorrect or no response

Conversion Chart:

Points	1	2	3	4	5	6	7	8	9	10	11	12	13	14	15	16
%	6	13	19	25	31	38	44	50	56	63	69	75	81	88	94	100

Name _____ Date _____ **Chapter 2**

Student Profile and Answer Key **Chapter Test** continued

How Are Rocks Alike and Different?

Directions: To determine how the student performed by objective, use the answer key on the previous page to find the student's score for each item. In the table below, circle the item number for each correct item, and write the number of points awarded for the constructed-response items. Total the score for each row to see the number correct for that objective.

Student Profile By Objective

Objective Code	Objective	Item Number	Score
02.10.01	Recognize that there are many different kinds of rocks.	8	____/1
02.10.02	Define rocks and minerals.	2	____/1
02.10.03	Recognize that most rocks are made of minerals.	14	____/1
02.10.04	Identify and compare properties of rocks.	4	____/1
02.10.05	Identify color and streak as properties of minerals.	5	____/1
02.10.06	Identify hardness as a property of minerals.	6	____/1
02.10.07	Identify cleavage, magnetism, luster, and acid reaction as properties of minerals.	7	____/1
02.10.08	Recognize how technology and tools are used in science.	15 (____/2)	____/2
02.10.09	Explain how igneous rock is formed.	1	____/1
02.10.10	Describe the properties of igneous rock.	9	____/1
02.10.11	Explain how sedimentary rock is formed.	10	____/1
02.10.12	Describe the properties of sedimentary rock.	11	____/1
02.10.13	Explain how fossils can be used to tell about the past.	12	____/1
02.10.14	Explain how metamorphic rock is formed.	13	____/1
02.10.15	Describe the properties of metamorphic rock.	3	____/1

Name _____ Date _____ Chapter 3

Student Profile and Answer Key — Chapter Test

What Are Renewable and Nonrenewable Resources?

Directions: Use the answer key on this page to score the items in the chapter test. Assign 1 point for each correct answer for multiple-choice items. Score the constructed-response item with the rubric on this page. Write the student's score in the Score column. Total the score and find the % score using the conversion chart at the bottom of the page. The objectives and their codes are provided in the table on the next page.

Student Profile and Answer Key

Item Number	Answer Key	Score	Objective Code
1	B		02.11.06
2	D		02.11.01
3	B		02.11.02
4	A		02.11.03
5	D		02.11.04
6	B		02.11.05
7	A		02.11.07
8	B		02.11.08
9	D		02.11.09
10	C		02.11.10
11	C		02.11.11
12	A		02.11.12
13	B		02.11.14
14	C		02.11.15
15	C		02.11.16
16	see rubric	___/2	02.11.13

Overall Score ___ = ___%

Rubric

Item 16

2 points: Student indicates that no-till farming is when farmers do not plow the land each year and indicates that farmers use no-till farming to protect the soil from erosion by wind or water

1 point: Student indicates that no-till farming is when farmers do not plow the land each year or indicates that farmers use no-till farming to protect the soil from erosion by wind or water

0 points: Student gives incorrect or no response

Conversion Chart:

Points	1	2	3	4	5	6	7	8	9	10	11	12	13	14	15	16	17
%	6	12	18	24	29	35	41	47	53	59	65	71	76	82	88	94	100

Name _____ Date _____ Chapter 3

Student Profile and Answer Key — Chapter Test continued

What Are Renewable and Nonrenewable Resources?

Directions: To determine how the student performed by objective, use the answer key on the previous page to find the student's score for each item. In the table below, circle the item number for each correct item, and write the number of points awarded for the constructed-response items. Total the score for each row to see the number correct for that objective.

Student Profile By Objective

Objective Code	Objective	Item Number	Score
02.11.01	Identify renewable resources.	2	___/1
02.11.02	Define and identify natural resources.	3	___/1
02.11.03	Identify water as a renewable resource.	4	___/1
02.11.04	Identify living things as renewable resources.	5	___/1
02.11.05	Identify sunlight and air as renewable resources.	6	___/1
02.11.06	Identify nonrenewable resources.	1	___/1
02.11.07	Identify rocks as a nonrenewable resource.	7	___/1
02.11.08	Identify metals as nonrenewable resources.	8	___/1
02.11.09	Identify fossil fuels as nonrenewable resources.	9	___/1
02.11.10	Identify soil as a nonrenewable resource.	10	___/1
02.11.11	Identify and describe the components and properties of soil.	11	___/1
02.11.12	Identify ways humans affect Earth's natural resources.	12	___/1
02.11.13	Describe ways to help the environment, such as composting preventing soil erosion.	16 (___/2)	___/2
02.11.14	Describe ways to help the environment, such as water conservation.	13	___/1
02.11.15	Describe ways to help the environment, such as recycling rock and mineral resources.	14	___/1
02.11.16	Describe ways to help the environment, such as using less fossil fuels.	15	___/1

Name _____ Date _____   Chapter 4

Student Profile and Answer Key — Chapter Test

How Do Slow Processes Change Earth's Surface?

Directions: Use the answer key on this page to score the items in the chapter test. Assign 1 point for each correct answer for multiple-choice items. Score the constructed-response item with the rubric on this page. Write the student's score in the Score column. Total the score and find the % score using the conversion chart at the bottom of the page. The objectives and their codes are provided in the table on the next page.

Student Profile and Answer Key

Item Number	Answer Key	Score	Objective Code
1	C		02.12.02
2	C		02.12.03
3	B		02.12.05
4	D		02.12.06
5	C		02.12.07
6	A		02.12.15
7	A		02.12.08
8	B		02.12.09
9	B		02.12.04
10	A		02.12.11
11	C		02.12.12
12	B		02.12.13
13	D		02.12.01
14	D		02.12.14
15	B		02.12.16
16	see rubric	___/2	02.12.10

Overall Score ___ = ___%

Rubric

Item 16

2 points: Student explains how water causes erosion, such as rivers and ocean waves moving sediment, and how water causes deposition, such as rivers depositing sediment as they slow down/when they enter an ocean and forming deltas

1 point: Student explains how water causes erosion or deposition

0 points: Student gives incorrect or no response

Conversion Chart:

Points	1	2	3	4	5	6	7	8	9	10	11	12	13	14	15	16	17
%	6	12	18	24	29	35	41	47	53	59	65	71	76	82	88	94	100

Name _____ Date _____ **Chapter 4**

Student Profile and Answer Key | Chapter Test continued

How Do Slow Processes Change Earth's Surface?

Directions: To determine how the student performed by objective, use the answer key on the previous page to find the student's score for each item. In the table below, circle the item number for each correct item, and write the number of points awarded for the constructed-response items. Total the score for each row to see the number correct for that objective.

Student Profile By Objective

Objective Code	Objective	Item Number	Score
02.12.01	Describe that Earth's surface can change slowly.	13	___/1
02.12.02	Identify the major landforms on Earth's surface.	1	___/1
02.12.03	Identify and describe how weathering changes Earth's surface.	2	___/1
02.12.04	Define physical weathering.	9	___/1
02.12.05	Define chemical weathering.	3	___/1
02.12.06	Identify and describe weathering by wind.	4	___/1
02.12.07	Identify and describe weathering by water.	5	___/1
02.12.08	Identify and describe weathering by plants and ice.	7	___/1
02.12.09	Identify and describe how erosion and deposition change Earth's surface.	8	___/1
02.12.10	Define erosion and deposition.	16 (___/2)	___/2
02.12.11	Identify and describe erosion and deposition by wind.	10	___/1
02.12.12	Identify and describe erosion and deposition by water.	11	___/1
02.12.13	Identify and describe erosion and deposition by ice.	12	___/1
02.12.14	Identify how weathering, erosion, and deposition affect people.	14	___/1
02.12.15	Identify and describe how weathering, erosion, and deposition can cause sinkholes and landslides.	6	___/1
02.12.16	Identify ways weathering, erosion, and deposition change the land where people live.	15	___/1

Name _____ Date _____ Chapter 5

Student Profile and Answer Key — Chapter Test

What Changes Do Volcanoes and Earthquakes Cause?

Directions: Use the answer key on this page to score the items in the chapter test. Assign 1 point for each correct answer for multiple-choice items. Score the constructed-response item with the rubric on this page. Write the student's score in the Score column. Total the score and find the % score using the conversion chart at the bottom of the page. The objectives and their codes are provided in the table on the next page.

Student Profile and Answer Key

Item Number	Answer Key	Score	Objective Code
1	A		02.13.02
2	C		02.13.03
3	D		02.13.04
4	B		02.13.05
5	B		02.13.06
6	C		02.13.07
7	A		02.13.08
8	see rubric	___/2	02.13.01

Overall Score ___ = ___%

Rubric

Item 8

2 points: Student names a process that changes Earth's surface quickly, such as a volcano, earthquake, or landslide, and describes what changes result from that change, such as lava covering the land, cracks or uneven land, or rocks/dirt moving to lower places

1 point: Student names a process that changes Earth's surface quickly or describes what changes result from a quick change

0 points: Student gives incorrect or no response

Conversion Chart:

Points	1	2	3	4	5	6	7	8	9
%	11	22	33	44	56	67	78	89	100

Name _____ Date _____ Chapter 5

Student Profile and Answer Key Chapter Test continued

What Changes Do Volcanoes and Earthquakes Cause?

Directions: To determine how the student performed by objective, use the answer key on the previous page to find the student's score for each item. In the table below, circle the item number for each correct item, and write the number of points awarded for the constructed-response items. Total the score for each row to see the number correct for that objective.

Student Profile By Objective

Objective Code	Objective	Item Number	Score
02.13.01	Identify and describe how Earth's surface can change rapidly.	8 (___/2)	___/2
02.13.02	Explain that Earth is made up of layers and Earth's surface is divided into plates.	1	___/1
02.13.03	Identify plate movement as a cause of mountain building.	2	___/1
02.13.04	Explain why earthquakes happen.	3	___/1
02.13.05	Explain how earthquakes can change Earth's surface.	4	___/1
02.13.06	Explain why volcanoes occur.	5	___/1
02.13.07	Explain how volcanoes can change Earth's surface.	6	___/1
02.13.08	Explain why landslides happen and how they change Earth's surface.	7	___/1

Name _____ Date _____   Chapter 6

Student Profile and Answer Key — Chapter Test

What Can We Observe About Weather?

Directions: Use the answer key on this page to score the items in the chapter test. Assign 1 point for each correct answer for multiple-choice items. Score the constructed-response item with the rubric on this page. Write the student's score in the Score column. Total the score and find the % score using the conversion chart at the bottom of the page. The objectives and their codes are provided in the table on the next page.

Student Profile and Answer Key

Item Number	Answer Key	Score	Objective Code
1	B		02.14.02
2	C		02.14.03
3	D		02.14.04
4	B		02.14.05
5	C		02.14.06
6	B		02.14.07
7	C		02.14.08
8	A		02.14.09
9	A		02.14.10
10	D		02.14.11
11	C		02.14.12
12	A		02.14.13
13	D		02.14.14
14	see rubric	___/2	02.14.01

Overall Score   ___ = ___%

Rubric

Item 14

2 points: Student states that the temperature will fall and the air pressure will fall

1 point: Student states that the temperature will fall or the air pressure will fall

0 points: Student gives incorrect or no response

Conversion Chart:

Points	1	2	3	4	5	6	7	8	9	10	11	12	13	14	15
%	7	13	20	27	33	40	47	53	60	67	73	80	87	93	100

Name _____ Date _____ Chapter 6

Student Profile and Answer Key — **Chapter Test** continued

What Can We Observe About Weather?

Directions: To determine how the student performed by objective, use the answer key on the previous page to find the student's score for each item. In the table below, circle the item number for each correct item, and write the number of points awarded for the constructed-response items. Total the score for each row to see the number correct for that objective.

Student Profile By Objective

Objective Code	Objective	Item Number	Score
02.14.01	Identify and describe weather changes and patterns by measurable quantities.	14 (___/2)	___/2
02.14.02	Explain that air surrounds us and takes up space.	1	___/1
02.14.03	Identify and describe the layers of the atmosphere.	2	___/1
02.14.04	Identify and describe temperature and precipitation as measurable quantities of weather.	3	___/1
02.14.05	Identify and describe air pressure as measurable quantities of weather.	4	___/1
02.14.06	Identify and describe wind and humidity as measurable quantities of weather.	5	___/1
02.14.07	Describe how water exists in the air and how clouds form.	6	___/1
02.14.08	Identify and describe cumulus clouds.	7	___/1
02.14.09	Identify and describe stratus clouds.	8	___/1
02.14.10	Identify and describe cirrus clouds.	9	___/1
02.14.11	Identify and describe how air masses affect weather.	10	___/1
02.14.12	Identify and describe how cold fronts affect weather.	11	___/1
02.14.13	Identify and describe how warm fronts affect weather.	12	___/1
02.14.14	Identify and describe weather patterns that affect the United States.	13	___/1

Name _____ Date _____

Earth Science

Student Profile and Answer Key — Benchmark Test

Directions: Use the answer key on this page to score the items in the benchmark test. Assign 1 point for each correct answer for multiple-choice items. Score the constructed-response items with the rubrics on this page. Write the student's score in the Score column. Total the score and calculate the % score. The objectives and their codes are provided in a table on the next page.

Student Profile and Answer Key

Item Number	Answer Key	Score	Objective Code
1	D		02.11.01
2	A		02.09.02
3	A		02.09.07
4	B		02.09.08
5	D		02.09.14
6	B		02.10.04
7	D		02.10.07
8	D		02.10.13
9	A		02.11.06
10	B		02.11.11
11	B		02.11.12
12	C		02.12.02
13	B		02.12.03
14	A		02.12.09
15	A		02.12.14
16	D		02.09.01
17	C		02.13.02
18	C		02.13.05
19	D		02.13.07
20	B		02.14.01
21	D		02.14.02
22	see rubric	____/2	02.14.07
23	see rubric	____/2	02.13.01

Overall Score ____ x 4 = ____%

Rubric

Item 22

2 points: Student writes water vapor or a gas and states that water condenses and gathers around dust particles to form clouds

1 point: Student writes water vapor or a gas, or student states that water condenses and gathers around dust particles to form clouds particles to form clouds

0 points: Student gives incorrect or no response

Item 23

2 points: Student identifies a rapid change (earthquake, volcanic eruption, or landslide) and describes the geological forces that cause this change (plate movement, magma rising through weak spots, or any powerful movement including earthquakes, volcanic eruptions, or weathering)

1 point: Student identifies a rapid change but does not correctly explain what causes it

0 points: Student gives incorrect or no response

Name _____ Date _____ **Earth Science**

Student Profile and Answer Key — Benchmark Test continued

Directions: To determine how the student performed by objective, use the answer key on the previous page to find the student's score for each item. In the table below, circle the item number for each correct item, and write the number of points awarded for the constructed-response items. Total the score for each row to see the number correct for that objective.

Student Profile By Objective

Objective Code	Objective	Item Number	Score
02.09.01	Identify the movements of Earth and the moon.	16	___/1
02.09.02	Compare and contrast the characteristics of the sun, moon, and Earth.	2	___/1
02.09.07	Describe the orbit of Earth around the sun as it defines a year.	3	___/1
02.09.08	Explain that Earth's movement and position cause the seasons.	4	___/1
02.09.14	Describe the motion of the moon around Earth.	5	___/1
02.10.04	Identify and compare properties of rocks.	6	___/1
02.10.07	Identify cleavage, magnetism, luster, and acid reaction as properties of minerals.	7	___/1
02.10.13	Explain how fossils can be used to tell about the past.	8	___/1
02.11.01	Identify renewable resources.	1	___/1
02.11.06	Identify nonrenewable resources.	9	___/1
02.11.11	Identify and describe the components and properties of soil.	10	___/1
02.11.12	Identify ways humans affect Earth's natural resources.	11	___/1
02.12.02	Identify the major landforms on Earth's surface.	12	___/1
02.12.03	Identify and describe how weathering changes Earth's surface.	13	___/1
02.12.09	Identify and describe how erosion and deposition change Earth's surface.	14	___/1
02.12.14	Identify how weathering, erosion, and deposition affect people.	15	___/1
02.13.01	Identify and describe how Earth's surface can change rapidly.	23 (___/2)	___/2
02.13.02	Explain that Earth is made up of layers and Earth's surface is divided into plates.	17	___/1
02.13.05	Explain how earthquakes can change Earth's surface.	18	___/1
02.13.07	Explain how volcanoes can change Earth's surface.	19	___/1
02.14.01	Identify and describe weather changes and patterns by measurable quantities.	20	___/1
02.14.02	Explain that air surrounds us and takes up space.	21	___/1
02.14.07	Describe how water exists in the air and how clouds form.	22 (___/2)	___/2

Class Profile — Earth Science

Directions: Write student names below. Record student Chapter Test and Benchmark Test scores in the columns to the right.

Student Name	Chapter Test 1	Chapter Test 2	Chapter Test 3	Chapter Test 4	Chapter Test 5	Chapter Test 6	Benchmark Test

Name _____ Date _____ **Chapter 1**

Student Profile and Answer Key — Chapter Test

How Can You Describe and Measure Properties of Matter?

Directions: Use the answer key on this page to score the items in the chapter test. Assign 1 point for each correct answer for multiple-choice items. Score the constructed-response item with the rubric on this page. Write the student's score in the Score column. Total the score and find the % score using the conversion chart at the bottom of the page. The objectives and their codes are provided in the table on the next page.

Student Profile and Answer Key

Item Number	Answer Key	Score	Objective Code
1	B		03.06.02
2	B		03.06.01
3	A		03.06.03
4	D		03.06.04
5	A		03.06.05
6	B		03.06.06
7	C		03.06.13
8	C		03.06.09
9	D		03.06.10
10	A		03.06.11
11	A		03.06.12
12	D		03.06.08
13	C		03.06.14
14	C		03.06.15
15	A		03.06.16
16	see rubric	___/2	03.06.07

Overall Score   ___ = ___%

Rubric

Item 16

2 points: Student states that the groups used different properties for their sorts and that Group 1 sorted by shape and Group 2 sorted by magnetism

1 point: Student states that the groups used different properties for their sorts or that Group 1 sorted by shape and Group 2 sorted by magnetism

0 points: Student gives incorrect or no response

Conversion Chart:

Points	1	2	3	4	5	6	7	8	9	10	11	12	13	14	15	16	17
%	6	12	18	24	29	35	41	47	53	59	65	71	76	82	88	94	100

Name _____ Date _____ Chapter 1

Student Profile and Answer Key — Chapter Test continued

How Can You Describe and Measure Properties of Matter?

Directions: To determine how the student performed by objective, use the answer key on the previous page to find the student's score for each item. In the table below, circle the item number for each correct item, and write the number of points awarded for the constructed-response items. Total the score for each row to see the number correct for that objective.

Student Profile By Objective

Objective Code	Objective	Item Number	Score
03.06.01	Understand that all objects and substances in the world are made of matter.	2	___/1
03.06.02	Recognize that matter has properties that can be observed through the senses.	1	___/1
03.06.03	Recognize that matter takes up space and has mass.	3	___/1
03.06.04	Understand that two objects cannot occupy the same place at the same time.	4	___/1
03.06.05	Recognize that some properties of an object are dependent on the conditions of the present surroundings in which the object exists.	5	___/1
03.06.06	Understand that materials may be composed of parts too small to be seen without magnification and that matter may be classified based on qualities that can only be observed with magnification.	6	___/1
03.06.07	Classify types of materials or mixtures of substances by using their characteristic properties.	16 (___/2)	___/2
03.06.08	Observe and describe that mixtures are made by combining solids or liquids or a combination.	12	___/1
03.06.09	Distinguish between the components in a mixture or solution.	8	___/1
03.06.10	Describe ways to separate the components of a mixture/solution by their properties.	9	___/1
03.06.11	Identify that water can dissolve some materials.	10	___/1
03.06.12	Understand that measurements can be made with standard metric units and nonstandard units.	11	___/1
03.06.13	Recognize that matter can be observed or measured with tools such as hand lenses, metric rulers, thermometers, balances, magnets, circuit testers, and graduated cylinders.	7	___/1
03.06.14	Measure the weight (spring scale) and mass (balances in grams or kilograms) of objects.	13	___/1
03.06.15	Observe that the total mass of a material remains constant whether it is together, in parts, or in a different state.	14	___/1
03.06.16	Describe and compare the volumes of objects using a graduated cylinder.	15	___/1

Name _____ Date _____ **Chapter 2**

Student Profile and Answer Key | Chapter Test

What Are Physical and Chemical Changes?

Directions: Use the answer key on this page to score the items in the chapter test. Assign 1 point for each correct answer for multiple-choice items. Score the constructed-response item with the rubric on this page. Write the student's score in the Score column. Total the score and find the % score using the conversion chart at the bottom of the page. The objectives and their codes are provided in the table on the next page.

Student Profile and Answer Key

Item Number	Answer Key	Score	Objective Code
1	B		03.07.05
2	C		03.07.01
3	B		03.07.02
4	D		03.07.03
5	see rubric	___/2	03.07.04
Overall Score		___ = ___%	

Rubric

Item 5

2 points: Student states two differences between liquid and solid states of water, such as liquid taking the shape of its container and solid keeping its shape or liquid and solid water existing at different temperature ranges

1 point: Student state one difference between liquid and solid states of water

0 points: Student gives incorrect or no response

Conversion Chart:

Points	1	2	3	4	5	6
%	17	33	50	67	83	100

Grade 4 Assessment

Name _____ Date _____   Chapter 2

Student Profile and Answer Key — Chapter Test continued

What Are Physical and Chemical Changes?

Directions: To determine how the student performed by objective, use the answer key on the previous page to find the student's score for each item. In the table below, circle the item number for each correct item, and write the number of points awarded for the constructed-response items. Total the score for each row to see the number correct for that objective.

Student Profile By Objective

Objective Code	Objective	Item Number	Score
03.07.01	Explain how matter can change from one state to another by heating and cooling.	2	___/1
03.07.02	Understand that, when a new material is made by combining two or more materials, it has properties that are different from the original materials.	3	___/1
03.07.03	Observe and describe changes in the properties of materials or objects.	4	___/1
03.07.04	Compare and contrast the states of matter.	5 (___/2)	___/2
03.07.05	Realize that water has unique properties that make it an important resource.	1	___/1

Name _____ Date _____ Chapter 3

Student Profile and Answer Key — Chapter Test

How Do Forces Act?

Directions: Use the answer key on this page to score the items in the chapter test. Assign 1 point for each correct answer for multiple-choice items. Score the constructed-response item with the rubric on this page. Write the student's score in the Score column. Total the score and find the % score using the conversion chart at the bottom of the page. The objectives and their codes are provided in the table on the next page.

Student Profile and Answer Key

Item Number	Answer Key	Score	Objective Code
1	C		03.08.01
2	D		03.08.02
3	D		03.08.03
4	A		03.08.04
5	B		03.08.05
6	D		03.08.06
7	A		03.08.07
8	A		03.08.08
9	C		03.08.09
10	B		03.08.10
11	D		03.08.11
12	see rubric	___/2	03.08.12

Overall Score ___ = ___%

Rubric

Item 12

2 points: Student states that weight is the measure of gravity's pull on an object

1 point: Student mentions measuring or gravity but does not correctly connect the two or confuses with mass or heaviness

0 points: Student gives incorrect or no response

Conversion Chart:

Points	1	2	3	4	5	6	7	8	9	10	11	12	13
%	8	15	23	31	38	46	54	62	69	77	85	92	100

Name _____ Date _____ **Chapter 3**

Student Profile and Answer Key — Chapter Test continued

How Do Forces Act?

Directions: To determine how the student performed by objective, use the answer key on the previous page to find the student's score for each item. In the table below, circle the item number for each correct item, and write the number of points awarded for the constructed-response items. Total the score for each row to see the number correct for that objective.

Student Profile By Objective

Objective Code	Objective	Item Number	Score
03.08.01	Identify forces as pushes and pulls.	1	___/1
03.08.02	Explain that forces cause motion.	2	___/1
03.08.03	Describe that if forces are applied to an object that does not move, the forces being applied are equal.	3	___/1
03.08.04	Explain that objects move because unequal forces are applied to the objects.	4	___/1
03.08.05	Describe that the greater the mass of an object, the greater the force needed to move that object.	5	___/1
03.08.06	Describe that forces can change the direction of an object.	6	___/1
03.08.07	Explain that the greater the force applied to an object, the greater the change in an object's motion.	7	___/1
03.08.08	Explain that objects can move in different ways.	8	___/1
03.08.09	Explain that the speed of an object depends on the time it takes the object to move a certain distance.	9	___/1
03.08.10	Define friction as a force that slows motion when objects are touching.	10	___/1
03.08.11	Identify gravity as a force that pulls objects toward the center of Earth.	11	___/1
03.08.12	Explain that weight is the measure of the Earth's pull on an object.	12 (___/2)	___/2

Name _____ Date _____ Chapter 4

Student Profile and Answer Key — Chapter Test

What Is Magnetism?

Directions: Use the answer key on this page to score the items in the chapter test. Assign 1 point for each correct answer for multiple-choice items. Score the constructed-response item with the rubric on this page. Write the student's score in the Score column. Total the score and find the % score using the conversion chart at the bottom of the page. The objectives and their codes are provided in the table on the next page.

Student Profile and Answer Key

Item Number	Answer Key	Score	Objective Code
1	B		03.09.03
2	A		03.09.01
3	A		03.09.04
4	D		03.09.05
5	B		03.09.06
6	see rubric	___/2	03.09.02
Overall Score		___ = ___%	

Rubric

Item 6

2 points: Student states that the piece of paper is not magnetic and that the paper clip is made from magnetic material (iron, nickel, or cobalt)

1 point: Student states that the piece of paper is not magnetic or that the paper clip is made from magnetic material (iron, nickel, or cobalt)

0 points: Student gives incorrect or no response

Conversion Chart:

Points	1	2	3	4	5	6	7
%	14	29	43	57	71	86	100

Name _____ Date _____ Chapter 4

Student Profile and Answer Key — **Chapter Test** continued

What Is Magnetism?

Directions: To determine how the student performed by objective, use the answer key on the previous page to find the student's score for each item. In the table below, circle the item number for each correct item, and write the number of points awarded for the constructed-response items. Total the score for each row to see the number correct for that objective.

Student Profile By Objective

Objective Code	Objective	Item Number	Score
03.09.01	Identify magnets and how they function in everyday life.	2	___/1
03.09.02	Describe that magnets can attract magnetic materials.	6 (___/2)	___/2
03.09.03	Describe that magnets can attract and repel other magnets.	1	___/1
03.09.04	Classify materials as magnetic and non-magnetic.	3	___/1
03.09.05	Describe the effects of a magnetic field.	4	___/1
03.09.06	Explain that the force of magnetism decreases as distance increases.	5	___/1

Name _____ Date _____   Chapter 5

Student Profile and Answer Key Chapter Test

What Are Some Forms of Energy?

Directions: Use the answer key on this page to score the items in the chapter test. Assign 1 point for each correct answer for multiple-choice items. Score the constructed-response item with the rubric on this page. Write the student's score in the Score column. Total the score and find the % score using the conversion chart at the bottom of the page. The objectives and their codes are provided in the table on the next page.

Student Profile and Answer Key

Item Number	Answer Key	Score	Objective Code
1	C		03.10.03
2	A		03.10.01
3	D		03.10.02
4	B		03.10.04
5	C		03.10.05
6	D		03.10.06
7	B		03.10.07
8	C		03.10.09
9	see rubric	___/2	03.10.08

Overall Score ___ = ___%

Rubric

Item 9

- *2 points:* Student gives examples of a material that reflects light and a material that lets light pass through and explains that light bounces off the reflective material and passes through the other material

- *1 point:* Student gives examples of a material that reflects light and a material that lets light pass through or explains that light bounces off some materials and passes through other materials

- *0 points:* Student gives incorrect or no response

Conversion Chart:

Points	1	2	3	4	5	6	7	8	9	10
%	10	20	30	40	50	60	70	80	90	100

Name _____ Date _____ **Chapter 5**

Student Profile and Answer Key — Chapter Test continued

What Are Some Forms of Energy?

Directions: To determine how the student performed by objective, use the answer key on the previous page to find the student's score for each item. In the table below, circle the item number for each correct item, and write the number of points awarded for the constructed-response items. Total the score for each row to see the number correct for that objective.

Student Profile By Objective

Objective Code	Objective	Item Number	Score
03.10.01	Describe motion as the result of energy being used.	2	___/1
03.10.02	Define energy as the source of motion or change.	3	___/1
03.10.03	Identify and describe heat as the flow of energy from a warmer object to a cooler object.	1	___/1
03.10.04	Describe that heat flows between objects until they are both the same temperature.	4	___/1
03.10.05	Describe heat as the energy produced when substances burn or certain kinds of materials rub against each other.	5	___/1
03.10.06	Identify common materials that conduct heat well or poorly.	6	___/1
03.10.07	Identify and describe light as a form of energy.	7	___/1
03.10.08	Explain that light can be reflected from some objects and pass through other objects.	9 (___/2)	___/2
03.10.09	Identify and describe chemical energy as a form of energy.	8	___/1

Name _____ Date _____

Chapter 6

Student Profile and Answer Key — Chapter Test

What Is Sound?

Directions: Use the answer key on this page to score the items in the chapter test. Assign 1 point for each correct answer for multiple-choice items. Score the constructed-response item with the rubric on this page. Write the student's score in the Score column. Total the score and find the % score using the conversion chart at the bottom of the page. The objectives and their codes are provided in the table on the next page.

Student Profile and Answer Key

Item Number	Answer Key	Score	Objective Code
1	D		03.11.02
2	A		03.11.01
3	C		03.11.03
4	see rubric	___/2	03.11.04
Overall Score		___ = ___%	

Rubric

Item 4

- *2 points:* Student writes flute and connects smaller instruments, faster vibrations, and higher pitch
- *1 point:* Student writes flute or connects smaller instruments, faster vibrations, and higher pitch
- *0 points:* Student gives incorrect or no response

Conversion Chart:

Points	1	2	3	4	5
%	20	40	60	80	100

Name _____ Date _____ Chapter 6

Student Profile and Answer Key — Chapter Test continued

What Is Sound?

Directions: To determine how the student performed by objective, use the answer key on the previous page to find the student's score for each item. In the table below, circle the item number for each correct item, and write the number of points awarded for the constructed-response items. Total the score for each row to see the number correct for that objective.

Student Profile By Objective

Objective Code	Objective	Item Number	Score
03.11.01	Understand that energy exists in various forms, including sound.	2	___/1
03.11.02	Recognize that vibrating objects make sound, and sound can make things vibrate.	1	___/1
03.11.03	Understand the relationship between volume and vibrations.	3	___/1
03.11.04	Understand that pitch is caused by vibrations. The faster the vibrations, the higher the pitch.	4 (___/2)	___/2

Grade 4 Assessment

Name _____ Date _____ Chapter 7

Student Profile and Answer Key — Chapter Test

What Is Electricity?

Directions: Use the answer key on this page to score the items in the chapter test. Assign 1 point for each correct answer for multiple-choice items. Score the constructed-response item with the rubric on this page. Write the student's score in the Score column. Total the score and find the % score using the conversion chart at the bottom of the page. The objectives and their codes are provided in the table on the next page.

Student Profile and Answer Key

Item Number	Answer Key	Score	Objective Code
1	D		03.12.01
2	C		03.12.02
3	C		03.12.03
4	B		03.12.04
5	A		03.12.05
6	C		03.12.08
7	C		03.12.06
8	see rubric	___/2	03.12.07

Overall Score   ___ = ___%

Rubric

Item 8

- *2 points:* Student states that the paper clips will become attached to the magnet when the circuit is closed and that they will fall off when the circuit is open
- *1 point:* Student states that the paper clips will become attached to the magnet when the circuit is closed or that they will fall off when the circuit is open
- *0 points:* Student gives incorrect or no response

Conversion Chart:

Points	1	2	3	4	5	6	7	8	9
%	11	22	33	44	56	67	78	89	100

Name _____ Date _____ Chapter 7

Student Profile and Answer Key — Chapter Test continued

What Is Electricity?

Directions: To determine how the student performed by objective, use the answer key on the previous page to find the student's score for each item. In the table below, circle the item number for each correct item, and write the number of points awarded for the constructed-response items. Total the score for each row to see the number correct for that objective.

Student Profile By Objective

Objective Code	Objective	Item Number	Score
03.12.01	Understand that electric circuits may produce or use light, heat, sound, and magnetic energy.	1	___/1
03.12.02	Observe and predict the effects of static electricity on the motion of objects.	2	___/1
03.12.03	Demonstrate how electrical energy is transferred and changed through the use of a simple circuit.	3	___/1
03.12.04	Classify objects that are good conductors or poor conductors of electricity.	4	___/1
03.12.05	Recognize that a simple circuit must be closed to conduct electricity.	5	___/1
03.12.06	Understand that magnets and electricity produce related forces.	7	___/1
03.12.07	Realize that electric charges flowing through a wire can produce a measurable force on magnets and other objects.	8 (___/2)	___/2
03.12.08	Compare and contrast simple and parallel circuits.	6	___/1

Name _____ Date _____ **Physical Science**

Student Profile and Answer Key — Benchmark Test

Directions: Use the answer key on this page to score the items in the benchmark test. Assign 1 point for each correct answer for multiple-choice items. Score the constructed-response items with the rubrics on this page. Write the student's score in the Score column. Total the score and calculate the % score. The objectives and their codes are provided in a table on the next page.

Student Profile and Answer Key

Item Number	Answer Key	Score	Objective Code
1	D		03.09.04
2	C		03.06.01
3	C		03.06.03
4	D		03.06.06
5	B		03.06.07
6	A		03.06.13
7	A		03.07.01
8	B		03.07.02
9	A		03.08.02
10	A		03.08.05
11	B		03.08.07
12	C		03.08.11
13	B		03.09.01
14	A		03.11.02
15	D		03.10.03
16	A		03.10.07
17	C		03.11.03
18	C		03.12.01
19	D		03.12.03
20	B		03.11.04
21	D		03.12.07
22	see rubric	___/2	03.10.02
23	see rubric	___/2	03.12.08

Overall Score ___ x 4 = ___ %

Rubric

Item 22

2 points: Student defines energy as the source of motion or change and gives one example of energy with an explanation of how it fits the definition

1 point: Student defines energy as the source of motion or change, or student gives one example of energy with an explanation of why it is energy

0 points: Student gives incorrect or no response

Item 23

2 points: Student identifies Circuit 1 as a series circuit and Circuit 2 as a parallel circuit and explains that if a bulb went out in Circuit 1, the rest of the bulbs would go out and if a bulb went out in Circuit 2, the rest of the bulbs would remain lit

1 point: Student identifies Circuit 1 as a series circuit and Circuit 2 as a parallel circuit or explains that if a bulb went out in Circuit 1, the rest of the bulbs would go out and if a bulb went out in Circuit 2, the rest of the bulbs would remain lit

0 points: Student gives incorrect or no response

Name _____ Date _____ **Physical Science**

Student Profile and Answer Key — Benchmark Test continued

Directions: To determine how the student performed by objective, use the answer key on the previous page to find the student's score for each item. In the table below, circle the item number for each correct item, and write the number of points awarded for the constructed-response items. Total the score for each row to see the number correct for that objective.

Student Profile By Objective

Objective Code	Objective	Item Number	Score
03.06.01	Understand that all objects and substances in the world are made of matter.	2	___/1
03.06.03	Recognize that matter takes up space and has mass.	3	___/1
03.06.06	Understand that materials may be composed of parts too small to be seen without magnification and that matter may be classified based on qualities that can only be observed with magnification.	4	___/1
03.06.07	Classify types of materials or mixtures of substances by using their characteristic properties.	5	___/1
03.06.13	Recognize that matter can be observed or measured with tools such as hand lenses, metric rulers, thermometers, balances, magnets, circuit testers, and graduated cylinders.	6	___/1
03.07.01	Explain how matter can change from one state to another by heating and cooling.	7	___/1
03.07.02	Understand that, when a new material is made by combining two or more materials, it has properties that are different from the original materials.	8	___/1
03.08.02	Explain that forces cause motion.	9	___/1
03.08.05	Describe that the greater the mass of an object, the greater the force needed to move that object.	10	___/1
03.08.07	Explain that the greater the force applied to an object, the greater the change in an object's motion.	11	___/1
03.08.11	Identify gravity as a force that pulls objects toward the center of Earth.	12	___/1
03.09.01	Identify magnets and how they function in everyday life.	13	___/1
03.09.04	Classify materials as magnetic and non-magnetic.	1	___/1
03.10.02	Define energy as the source of motion or change.	22 (___/2)	___/2
03.10.03	Identify and describe heat as the flow of energy from a warmer object to a cooler object.	15	___/1
03.10.07	Identify and describe light as a form of energy.	16	___/1
03.11.02	Recognize that vibrating objects make sound, and sound can make things vibrate.	14	___/1
03.11.03	Understand the relationship between volume and vibrations.	17	___/1
03.11.04	Understand that pitch is caused by vibrations. The faster the vibrations, the higher the pitch.	20	___/1
03.12.01	Understand that electric circuits may produce or use light, heat, sound, and magnetic energy.	18	___/1
03.12.03	Demonstrate how electrical energy is transferred and changed through the use of a simple circuit.	19	___/1
03.12.07	Realize that electric charges flowing through a wire can produce a measurable force on magnets and other objects.	21	___/1
03.12.08	Compare and contrast simple and parallel circuits.	23 (___/2)	___/2

Class Profile — Physical Science

Directions: Write student names below. Record student Chapter Test and Benchmark Test scores in the columns to the right.

Student Name	Chapter Test 1	Chapter Test 2	Chapter Test 3	Chapter Test 4	Chapter Test 5	Chapter Test 6	Chapter Test 7	Benchmark Test

Inquiry Rubrics and Self-Reflections

Life Science Rubrics	182
Life Science Self-Reflections	189
Earth Science Rubrics	202
Earth Science Self-Reflections	209
Physical Science Rubrics	222
Physical Science Self-Reflections	230

Inquiry Rubrics

Purpose and Description

Inquiry Rubrics are provided for scoring each of the Inquiry activities from the Science Inquiry Book of the Life Science, Earth Science, and Physical Science units. Each Inquiry Rubric is specific to the activity and lists the skills that students will demonstrate in that activity.

Make a copy of the rubric pages for each student. Evaluate each student after completing an activity. Assign 1 to 4 points for the student's performance on each of the skills, and then assign an overall score. Record the scores on each student's copy of the rubric.

Inquiry Self-Reflections

Purpose and Description

The Inquiry Self-Reflection, written in student-friendly, accessible language, helps students evaluate what they have learned by doing each activity. It allows students to review their own progress toward meeting specific skill goals. Students indicate their progress in attaining activity-specific skills. In addition, students are asked how well their group worked together, what went well or could be improved, and/or what was most memorable.

Make a copy of each Inquiry Self-Reflection for each student. After finishing each activity, ask students to complete the form. You may read the Inquiry Self-Reflection statements and questions aloud to the class if needed.

Name _____   Chapter 1

Inquiry Rubrics Life Science

Explore Activity   Date _____

Directions: Use the scale descriptions next to the table to guide your assessment of the student's work. Assess each item separately, and then decide on one overall score. Circle the score for each item and the overall score.

Inquiry Rubric	Scale			
The student planted radish seeds and **observed** them as they grew.	4	3	2	1
The student collected and recorded **data** about the life cycle of a radish plant.	4	3	2	1
The student **compared** the life cycles of radish plants and purple coneflowers.	4	3	2	1
The student compared observations and explained any variations.	4	3	2	1
The student **shared conclusions** about the life cycle of a radish plant.	4	3	2	1
Overall Score	4	3	2	1

Scale Descriptions

4: Student performs the skill with **thorough** understanding.
3: Student performs the skill with **adequate** understanding.
2: Student performs the skill with **basic** understanding.
1: Student performs the skill with **limited** understanding.

Directed Inquiry   Date _____

Directions: Use the scale descriptions next to the table to guide your assessment of the student's work. Assess each item separately, and then decide on one overall score. Circle the score for each item and the overall score.

Inquiry Rubric	Scale			
The student **observed** the parts of a flower using a hand lens and a microscope.	4	3	2	1
The student dissected a flower and identified each part.	4	3	2	1
The student **compared** the plant parts from different flowers.	4	3	2	1
The student collected **data** and **shared** results.	4	3	2	1
The student made an **inference** about how the structure of pollen aids in pollination and fertilization.	4	3	2	1
Overall Score	4	3	2	1

Scale Descriptions

4: Student performs the skill with **thorough** understanding.
3: Student performs the skill with **adequate** understanding.
2: Student performs the skill with **basic** understanding.
1: Student performs the skill with **limited** understanding.

Name _____   Chapter 2

Inquiry Rubrics — Life Science

Directed Inquiry
Date _____

Directions: Use the scale descriptions next to the table to guide your assessment of the student's work. Assess each item separately, and then decide on one overall score. Circle the score for each item and the overall score.

Inquiry Rubric	Scale
The student made a **prediction** about earthworm behavior in light and dark environments.	4 3 2 1
The student made **observations** about how the earthworms reacted to different environments.	4 3 2 1
The student repeated the trial several times and recorded any differences in observations.	4 3 2 1
The student **compared** data and observations from multiple trials.	4 3 2 1
The student made a **conclusion** about earthworm behavior.	4 3 2 1
Overall Score	4 3 2 1

Scale Descriptions
- 4: Student performs the skill with **thorough** understanding.
- 3: Student performs the skill with **adequate** understanding.
- 2: Student performs the skill with **basic** understanding.
- 1: Student performs the skill with **limited** understanding.

Guided Inquiry
Date _____

Directions: Use the scale descriptions next to the table to guide your assessment of the student's work. Assess each item separately, and then decide on one overall score. Circle the score for each item and the overall score.

Inquiry Rubric	Scale
The student recorded **observations** of butterfly growth and behavior.	4 3 2 1
The student made a diagram of a butterfly life cycle.	4 3 2 1
The student **compared** the life cycle of a butterfly with that of a grasshopper or a dragonfly.	4 3 2 1
The student compared observations and diagrams with other students.	4 3 2 1
The student **shared** results and **conclusions** with other students.	4 3 2 1
Overall Score	4 3 2 1

Scale Descriptions
- 4: Student performs the skill with **thorough** understanding.
- 3: Student performs the skill with **adequate** understanding.
- 2: Student performs the skill with **basic** understanding.
- 1: Student performs the skill with **limited** understanding.

Name _____   Chapter 3

Inquiry Rubrics — Life Science

Directed Inquiry
Date _____

Directions: Use the scale descriptions next to the table to guide your assessment of the student's work. Assess each item separately, and then decide on one overall score. Circle the score for each item and the overall score.

Inquiry Rubric	Scale			
The student **observed** and dissected an owl pellet.	4	3	2	1
The student collected **data** by **sorting** bones by type and counting the number of each type.	4	3	2	1
The student created a graph with data about the bones in the pellet.	4	3	2	1
The student **estimated** the number of animal remains in the pellet.	4	3	2	1
The student **shared conclusions** about owl pellets with other students.	4	3	2	1
Overall Score	4	3	2	1

Scale Descriptions

4: Student performs the skill with **thorough** understanding.
3: Student performs the skill with **adequate** understanding.
2: Student performs the skill with **basic** understanding.
1: Student performs the skill with **limited** understanding.

Guided Inquiry
Date _____

Directions: Use the scale descriptions next to the table to guide your assessment of the student's work. Assess each item separately, and then decide on one overall score. Circle the score for each item and the overall score.

Inquiry Rubric	Scale			
The student **observed** the bones and identified the animal to which the bones belonged.	4	3	2	1
The student sorted the bones and reconstructed the skeleton of an animal.	4	3	2	1
The student analyzed **data** and made a short food chain.	4	3	2	1
The student drew **conclusions** about the types of animals that owls eat.	4	3	2	1
The student **shared** and **compared** ideas with others to create a larger food web.	4	3	2	1
Overall Score	4	3	2	1

Scale Descriptions

4: Student performs the skill with **thorough** understanding.
3: Student performs the skill with **adequate** understanding.
2: Student performs the skill with **basic** understanding.
1: Student performs the skill with **limited** understanding.

Name _____   **Chapter 4**

Inquiry Rubrics — Life Science

Directed Inquiry

Date _____

Directions: Use the scale descriptions next to the table to guide your assessment of the student's work. Assess each item separately, and then decide on one overall score. Circle the score for each item and the overall score.

Inquiry Rubric	Scale				Scale Descriptions
The student **observed** a plant fossil, made rubbings, and recorded observations and information in a table.	4	3	2	1	4: Student performs the skill with **thorough** understanding.
The student **compared** the fossilized plant to a similar modern plant and with other fossils.	4	3	2	1	3: Student performs the skill with **adequate** understanding.
The student made **inferences** about the fossilized plant's environment.	4	3	2	1	2: Student performs the skill with **basic** understanding.
The student made a display to **share** results and **conclusions** with others.	4	3	2	1	1: Student performs the skill with **limited** understanding.
The student asked **questions** about the displays of others.	4	3	2	1	
Overall Score	4	3	2	1	

Guided Inquiry

Date _____

Directions: Use the scale descriptions next to the table to guide your assessment of the student's work. Assess each item separately, and then decide on one overall score. Circle the score for each item and the overall score.

Inquiry Rubric	Scale				Scale Descriptions
The student **investigated** how camouflage helps prey avoid being seen by predators.	4	3	2	1	4: Student performs the skill with **thorough** understanding.
The student used a **model** to make qualitative and quantitative **observations**.	4	3	2	1	3: Student performs the skill with **adequate** understanding.
The student recorded **data** in tables and graphs.	4	3	2	1	2: Student performs the skill with **basic** understanding.
The student **shared** and **compared** data from different trials and explained any differences.	4	3	2	1	1: Student performs the skill with **limited** understanding.
The student **inferred** how the adaptation of camouflage helps animals survive.	4	3	2	1	
Overall Score	4	3	2	1	

Name _____ Chapter 5

Inquiry Rubrics Life Science

Directed Inquiry Date _____

Directions: Use the scale descriptions next to the table to guide your assessment of the student's work. Assess each item separately, and then decide on one overall score. Circle the score for each item and the overall score.

Inquiry Rubric	Scale			
The student **observed** how water vapor released by the leaves of a plant cutting condensed on a cup.	4	3	2	1
The student collected **data** and recorded observations of the cup over several days.	4	3	2	1
The student **compared** observations with other students.	4	3	2	1
The student **inferred** what happened to the water that the plant cutting took in.	4	3	2	1
The student **shared conclusions** about how plants affect the environment.	4	3	2	1
Overall Score	4	3	2	1

Scale Descriptions

4: Student performs the skill with **thorough** understanding.
3: Student performs the skill with **adequate** understanding.
2: Student performs the skill with **basic** understanding.
1: Student performs the skill with **limited** understanding.

Guided Inquiry Date _____

Directions: Use the scale descriptions next to the table to guide your assessment of the student's work. Assess each item separately, and then decide on one overall score. Circle the score for each item and the overall score.

Inquiry Rubric	Scale			
The student made a **hypothesis** about the colors in a green leaf.	4	3	2	1
The student identified **variables** to change, to control, and to **observe**.	4	3	2	1
The student collected and recorded **data** and **compared** observations with others.	4	3	2	1
The student made **inferences** about why the filters showed several colors and why leaves of some trees change color.	4	3	2	1
The student **shared** results and compared ideas based on the evidence gathered in the investigation.	4	3	2	1
Overall Score	4	3	2	1

Scale Descriptions

4: Student performs the skill with **thorough** understanding.
3: Student performs the skill with **adequate** understanding.
2: Student performs the skill with **basic** understanding.
1: Student performs the skill with **limited** understanding.

Name _____   **Chapter 6**

Inquiry Rubrics — Life Science

Directed Inquiry

Date _____

Directions: Use the scale descriptions next to the table to guide your assessment of the student's work. Assess each item separately, and then decide on one overall score. Circle the score for each item and the overall score.

Inquiry Rubric	Scale				Scale Descriptions
The student **observed** what happened as the brain processed information.	4	3	2	1	4: Student performs the skill with **thorough** understanding.
The student **measured** how long it took his or her partner to read each test.	4	3	2	1	3: Student performs the skill with **adequate** understanding.
The student recorded **data** in a table.	4	3	2	1	2: Student performs the skill with **basic** understanding.
The student formed a **conclusion** about how the brain processes information based on observations and data.	4	3	2	1	1: Student performs the skill with **limited** understanding.
The student **shared** and **compared** data and conclusions with others.	4	3	2	1	
Overall Score	4	3	2	1	

Guided Inquiry

Date _____

Directions: Use the scale descriptions next to the table to guide your assessment of the student's work. Assess each item separately, and then decide on one overall score. Circle the score for each item and the overall score.

Inquiry Rubric	Scale				Scale Descriptions
The student made a **hypothesis** about how exercise would affect heart rate.	4	3	2	1	4: Student performs the skill with **thorough** understanding.
The student **planned** and conducted an **experiment**.	4	3	2	1	3: Student performs the skill with **adequate** understanding.
The student **measured** heart rate before and after exercising.	4	3	2	1	2: Student performs the skill with **basic** understanding.
The student formed a **conclusion** about how exercise affects heart rate.	4	3	2	1	1: Student performs the skill with **limited** understanding.
The student **shared** and **compared data** with other students.	4	3	2	1	
Overall Score	4	3	2	1	

Name _____

Inquiry Rubrics — Life Science

Open Inquiry

Date _____

Directions: Use the scale descriptions next to the table to guide your assessment of the student's work. Assess each item separately, and then decide on one overall score. Circle the score for each item and the overall score.

Inquiry Rubric	Scale
The student generated or chose a **question** to **investigate**.	4 3 2 1
The student planned an **experiment** by identifying, manipulating, and controlling **variables**.	4 3 2 1
The student made and **compared observations** and collected and recorded **data**.	4 3 2 1
The student formed a **conclusion** and explained results based on evidence from the collected data and observations.	4 3 2 1
The student **shared** observations and conclusions with other students.	4 3 2 1
Overall Score	4 3 2 1

Scale Descriptions

4: Student performs the skill with **thorough** understanding.

3: Student performs the skill with **adequate** understanding.

2: Student performs the skill with **basic** understanding.

1: Student performs the skill with **limited** understanding.

Name _____   **Chapter 1**

Explore Activity Self-Reflection — Life Science

Directions: Write a ✓ in the box to show the answer that is true for you.

	Yes	Not Yet
❶ I can plant radish seeds and observe them as they grow.		
❷ I can collect and record data about the life cycle of a radish plant.		
❸ I can compare the life cycles of radish plants and purple coneflowers.		
❹ I can compare observations and explain any variations.		
❺ I can share conclusions about the life cycle of a radish plant.		

Directions: Think about the things you have studied in this chapter. Then finish the sentence.

❻ What do you like best about your chart? _____

_____

_____

_____

❼ What will you remember most from this activity? _____

_____

_____

_____

Name _____

Chapter 1

Directed Inquiry Self-Reflection — Life Science

Directions: Write a ✓ in the box to show the answer that is true for you.

	Yes	Not Yet
❶ I can observe the parts of a flower using a hand lens and a microscope.		
❷ I can cut apart a flower and identify each part.		
❸ I can compare the plant parts from different flowers.		
❹ I can collect data and share results.		
❺ I can make an inference about how the structure of pollen helps pollination and fertilization.		

Directions: Think about the things you have studied in this chapter. Then finish the sentence.

❻ What did you do well? _____

_____

_____

_____

❼ What will you remember most from this activity? _____

_____

_____

_____

Name _____

Chapter 2

Directed Inquiry Self-Reflection — Life Science

Directions: Write a ✓ in the box to show the answer that is true for you.

	Yes	Not Yet
❶ I can make a prediction about earthworm behavior in light and dark environments.		
❷ I can make observations about how earthworms behave in different environments.		
❸ I can repeat a trial several times and record any differences in observations.		
❹ I can compare data and observations from multiple trials.		
❺ I can make a conclusion about earthworm behavior.		

Directions: Think about the things you have studied in this chapter. Then finish the sentence.

❻ How well did your group work together? _____

_____

_____

_____

❼ What did you do well? _____

_____

_____

_____

Name _____   **Chapter 2**

Guided Inquiry Self-Reflection — Life Science

Directions: Write a ✓ in the box to show the answer that is true for you.

	Yes	Not Yet
❶ I can record observations of butterfly growth and behavior.		
❷ I can make a diagram of a butterfly life cycle.		
❸ I can compare the life cycle of a butterfly with the life cycle of a grasshopper or a dragonfly.		
❹ I can compare observations and diagrams with other students.		
❺ I can share results and conclusions with other students.		

Directions: Think about the things you have studied in this chapter. Then finish the sentence.

❻ What do you like best about your diagram? _____

_____

_____

_____

❼ What will you remember to do in your next activity? _____

_____

_____

_____

Name _____

Chapter 3

Directed Inquiry Self-Reflection — Life Science

Directions: Write a ✓ in the box to show the answer that is true for you.

	Yes	Not Yet
❶ I can observe and pull apart an owl pellet.		
❷ I can collect data by sorting bones by type and counting the number of each type.		
❸ I can create a graph with data about the bones in the pellet.		
❹ I can estimate the number of animal remains in the pellet.		
❺ I can share conclusions about owl pellets with other students.		

Directions: Think about the things you have studied in this chapter. Then finish the sentence.

❻ How well did your group work together? _____

_____

_____

_____

❼ What could you do to help your group work together better? _____

_____

_____

_____

Grade 4 Assessment

Name _____ **Chapter 3**

Guided Inquiry Self-Reflection — Life Science

Directions: Write a ✓ in the box to show the answer that is true for you.

	Yes	Not Yet
❶ I can observe the bones and identify the type of animal.		
❷ I can sort the bones and put together the skeleton of an animal.		
❸ I can use data to make a short food chain.		
❹ I can draw conclusions about the types of animals that owls eat.		
❺ I can share and compare ideas with others to create a larger food web.		

Directions: Think about the things you have studied in this chapter. Then finish the sentence.

❻ What did you do well? _____

_____

_____

_____

_____

❼ What will you remember most from this activity? _____

_____

_____

_____

Name _____   **Chapter 4**

Directed Inquiry Self-Reflection — Life Science

Directions: Write a ✓ in the box to show the answer that is true for you.

	Yes	Not Yet
❶ I can observe a plant fossil, make rubbings, and record observations and information in a table.		
❷ I can compare a fossilized plant to a similar modern plant and with other fossils.		
❸ I can make inferences about a fossilized plant's environment.		
❹ I can make a display to share results and conclusions with other students.		
❺ I can ask questions about other students' displays.		

Directions: Think about the things you have studied in this chapter. Then finish the sentence.

❻ How well did your group work together? _____

_____

_____

_____

❼ How would you improve this activity? _____

_____

_____

_____

Name _____   Chapter 4

Guided Inquiry Self-Reflection — Life Science

Directions: Write a ✓ in the box to show the answer that is true for you.

	Yes	Not Yet
❶ I can investigate how camouflage helps prey avoid being seen by predators.		
❷ I can use a model to make observations.		
❸ I can record data in tables and graphs.		
❹ I can share and compare data from different trials and explain any differences.		
❺ I can infer how camouflage helps animals survive.		

Directions: Think about the things you have studied in this chapter. Then finish the sentence.

❻ How could you have recorded your observations more accurately? _____

_____

_____

_____

❼ How could groups better explain their observations to each other? _____

_____

_____

_____

Name _____

Chapter 5

Directed Inquiry Self-Reflection — Life Science

Directions: Write a ✓ in the box to show the answer that is true for you.

	Yes	Not Yet
1 I can observe how water vapor released by the leaves of a plant cutting condenses on a cup.		
2 I can collect data and record observations of the cup over several days.		
3 I can compare observations with other students.		
4 I can infer what happened to the water that the plant cutting took in.		
5 I can share conclusions about how plants affect the environment.		

Directions: Think about the things you have studied in this chapter. Then finish the sentence.

6 What do you like best about your chart? _____

_____

_____

_____

7 How would you improve this activity? _____

_____

_____

_____

Name _____ **Chapter 5**

Guided Inquiry Self-Reflection — Life Science

Directions: Write a ✓ in the box to show the answer that is true for you.

	Yes	Not Yet
❶ I can make a hypothesis about the colors in a green leaf.		
❷ I can identify variables to change, to control, and to observe.		
❸ I can collect and record data and compare observations with others.		
❹ I can make inferences about why the filters showed several colors and why leaves of some trees change color.		
❺ I can share results and compare ideas based on data from the investigation.		

Directions: Think about the things you have studied in this chapter. Then finish the sentence.

❻ What did you do well? _____

_____

_____

_____

❼ What will you remember most from this activity? _____

_____

_____

_____

Name _____   **Chapter 6**

Directed Inquiry Self-Reflection — Life Science

Directions: Write a ✓ in the box to show the answer that is true for you.

	Yes	Not Yet
❶ I can observe what happens as the brain processes information.		
❷ I can measure how long it takes my partner to read each test.		
❸ I can record data in a table.		
❹ I can form a conclusion about how the brain processes information based on observations and data.		
❺ I can share and compare data and conclusions with other students.		

Directions: Think about the things you have studied in this chapter. Then finish the sentence.

❻ How could you tell the difference between an observation, a prediction, and an inference? _____

_____

_____

_____

❼ What did you do well? _____

_____

_____

_____

Name _____ **Chapter 6**

Guided Inquiry Self-Reflection — Life Science

Directions: Write a ✓ in the box to show the answer that is true for you.

	Yes	Not Yet
❶ I can make a hypothesis about how exercise will affect heart rate.		
❷ I can plan and conduct an experiment.		
❸ I can measure heart rate before and after exercising.		
❹ I can form a conclusion about how exercise affects heart rate.		
❺ I can share and compare data with other students.		

Directions: Think about the things you have studied in this chapter. Then finish the sentence.

❻ What did you like best about your experiment? _____

_____

_____

_____

❼ What will you remember most from this experiment? _____

_____

_____

_____

Grade 4 Assessment

Name _____

Open Inquiry Self-Reflection — Life Science

Directions: Write a ✓ in the box to show the answer that is true for you.

	Yes	Not Yet
❶ I can think of or choose a question to investigate.		
❷ I can plan an investigation by identifying, changing, and controlling variables.		
❸ I can make and compare observations and collect and record data.		
❹ I can form a conclusion and explain results based on data and observations.		
❺ I can share observations and conclusions with other students.		

Directions: Think about the things you have studied in this unit. Then finish the sentence.

❻ What do you like best about your experiment? _____

_____

_____

_____

❼ What will you remember to do in your next activity? _____

_____

_____

_____

Name _____ Chapter 1

Inquiry Rubrics — Earth Science

Explore Activity

Date _____

Directions: Use the scale descriptions next to the table to guide your assessment of the student's work. Assess each item separately, and then decide on one overall score. Circle the score for each item and the overall score.

Inquiry Rubric	Scale
The student constructed a model of star movement and used it to make **observations**.	4 3 2 1
The student collected and recorded **data** about how stars appear to move.	4 3 2 1
The student **compared** constellations that are visible at different times of night and at the same time of night in different seasons.	4 3 2 1
The student compared his or her observations with those of other students.	4 3 2 1
The student **shared** observations and **conclusions**.	4 3 2 1
Overall Score	4 3 2 1

Scale Descriptions

4: Student performs the skill with **thorough** understanding.
3: Student performs the skill with **adequate** understanding.
2: Student performs the skill with **basic** understanding.
1: Student performs the skill with **limited** understanding.

Directed Inquiry

Date _____

Directions: Use the scale descriptions next to the table to guide your assessment of the student's work. Assess each item separately, and then decide on one overall score. Circle the score for each item and the overall score.

Inquiry Rubric	Scale
The student created a **model** of the phases of the moon.	4 3 2 1
The student **observed** the model and recorded how the model showed the phases of the moon.	4 3 2 1
The student found a pattern in the moon phases.	4 3 2 1
The student drew a **conclusion** about the cause of the moon's phases.	4 3 2 1
The student **shared** and **compared** observations and explanations with other students.	4 3 2 1
Overall Score	4 3 2 1

Scale Descriptions

4: Student performs the skill with **thorough** understanding.
3: Student performs the skill with **adequate** understanding.
2: Student performs the skill with **basic** understanding.
1: Student performs the skill with **limited** understanding.

Grade 4 Assessment

Name _____ Chapter 2

Inquiry Rubrics — Earth Science

Directed Inquiry

Date _____

Directions: Use the scale descriptions next to the table to guide your assessment of the student's work. Assess each item separately, and then decide on one overall score. Circle the score for each item and the overall score.

Inquiry Rubric	Scale
The student **observed** the color, luster, and streak of each mineral.	4 3 2 1
The student used the Mohs scale to observe the hardness of each mineral.	4 3 2 1
The student identified each mineral and **compared** the minerals.	4 3 2 1
The student described the properties that were most useful in identifying the minerals.	4 3 2 1
The student **shared** results and conclusions with other students.	4 3 2 1
Overall Score	4 3 2 1

Scale Descriptions

4: Student performs the skill with **thorough** understanding.

3: Student performs the skill with **adequate** understanding.

2: Student performs the skill with **basic** understanding.

1: Student performs the skill with **limited** understanding.

Guided Inquiry

Date _____

Directions: Use the scale descriptions next to the table to guide your assessment of the student's work. Assess each item separately, and then decide on one overall score. Circle the score for each item and the overall score.

Inquiry Rubric	Scale
The student collected and recorded **observations** of the rocks.	4 3 2 1
The student used physical properties to identify the rocks and **classify** the rocks as igneous, sedimentary, or metamorphic.	4 3 2 1
The student explained how rocks in each group were alike.	4 3 2 1
The student **compared** methods and classifications with other students.	4 3 2 1
The student **shared** and compared ideas with other students.	4 3 2 1
Overall Score	4 3 2 1

Scale Descriptions

4: Student performs the skill with **thorough** understanding.

3: Student performs the skill with **adequate** understanding.

2: Student performs the skill with **basic** understanding.

1: Student performs the skill with **limited** understanding.

Name _____   Chapter 3

Inquiry Rubrics — Earth Science

Directed Inquiry

Date _____

Directions: Use the scale descriptions next to the table to guide your assessment of the student's work. Assess each item separately, and then decide on one overall score. Circle the score for each item and the overall score.

Inquiry Rubric	Scale			
The student **observed** three different soil samples and **predicted** which would be best for growing a corn seedling.	4	3	2	1
The student **measured** the growth of seedlings and recorded observations and **data** in a table.	4	3	2	1
The student **compared** the prediction with the results.	4	3	2	1
The student **concluded** which soil had the highest fertility based on analyzed data and observations.	4	3	2	1
The student **shared** and compared observations and conclusions.	4	3	2	1
Overall Score	4	3	2	1

Scale Descriptions

4: Student performs the skill with **thorough** understanding.
3: Student performs the skill with **adequate** understanding.
2: Student performs the skill with **basic** understanding.
1: Student performs the skill with **limited** understanding.

Guided Inquiry

Date _____

Directions: Use the scale descriptions next to the table to guide your assessment of the student's work. Assess each item separately, and then decide on one overall score. Circle the score for each item and the overall score.

Inquiry Rubric	Scale			
The student **observed** and **classified** soils.	4	3	2	1
The student wrote a **hypothesis** about which soil would absorb more water.	4	3	2	1
The student **measured**, collected, and recorded **data** about soil absorption.	4	3	2	1
The student drew a **conclusion** about which soil absorbed more water.	4	3	2	1
The student **shared** and **compared** observations and conclusions with others.	4	3	2	1
Overall Score	4	3	2	1

Scale Descriptions

4: Student performs the skill with **thorough** understanding.
3: Student performs the skill with **adequate** understanding.
2: Student performs the skill with **basic** understanding.
1: Student performs the skill with **limited** understanding.

Name _____   **Chapter 4**

Inquiry Rubrics — Earth Science

Directed Inquiry

Date _____

Directions: Use the scale descriptions next to the table to guide your assessment of the student's work. Assess each item separately, and then decide on one overall score. Circle the score for each item and the overall score.

Inquiry Rubric	Scale			
The student **predicted** what would happen when sandstone is rubbed together and shaken in water.	4	3	2	1
The student **observed** models of physical weathering, chemical weathering, and erosion.	4	3	2	1
The student recorded observations and **compared** observations with others.	4	3	2	1
The student used the **models** to identify examples of physical weathering, chemical weathering, and erosion.	4	3	2	1
The student **shared conclusions** with other students.	4	3	2	1
Overall Score	4	3	2	1

Scale Descriptions

4: Student performs the skill with **thorough** understanding.
3: Student performs the skill with **adequate** understanding.
2: Student performs the skill with **basic** understanding.
1: Student performs the skill with **limited** understanding.

Guided Inquiry

Date _____

Directions: Use the scale descriptions next to the table to guide your assessment of the student's work. Assess each item separately, and then decide on one overall score. Circle the score for each item and the overall score.

Inquiry Rubric	Scale			
The student made a **hypothesis** about how water poured on soil affects the movement of soil.	4	3	2	1
The student carried out an **experiment** to test how water poured on soil affects the movement of soil.	4	3	2	1
The student made and **compared observations** and collected and recorded **data** about the amount of erosion when water is poured on soil at different rates.	4	3	2	1
The student formed a **conclusion** and explained results based on evidence from data and observations.	4	3	2	1
The student **shared** results with other students.	4	3	2	1
Overall Score	4	3	2	1

Scale Descriptions

4: Student performs the skill with **thorough** understanding.
3: Student performs the skill with **adequate** understanding.
2: Student performs the skill with **basic** understanding.
1: Student performs the skill with **limited** understanding.

Name _____   Chapter 5

Inquiry Rubrics | Earth Science

Directed Inquiry   Date _____

Directions: Use the scale descriptions next to the table to guide your assessment of the student's work. Assess each item separately, and then decide on one overall score. Circle the score for each item and the overall score.

Inquiry Rubric	Scale
The student built and used a **model** to learn more about earthquakes.	4 3 2 1
The student made **predictions** about the motion of the blocks.	4 3 2 1
The student understood and followed safety procedures.	4 3 2 1
The student **shared** methods, data, and results with other students.	4 3 2 1
The student drew **conclusions** about earthquakes based on the model.	4 3 2 1
Overall Score	4 3 2 1

Scale Descriptions

4: Student performs the skill with **thorough** understanding.

3: Student performs the skill with **adequate** understanding.

2: Student performs the skill with **basic** understanding.

1: Student performs the skill with **limited** understanding.

Guided Inquiry   Date _____

Directions: Use the scale descriptions next to the table to guide your assessment of the student's work. Assess each item separately, and then decide on one overall score. Circle the score for each item and the overall score.

Inquiry Rubric	Scale
The student used a **model** to investigate how some types of mountains form.	4 3 2 1
The student **predicted** how different amounts of force would change the model.	4 3 2 1
The student drew **conclusions** about how mountains form.	4 3 2 1
The student explained how the model was similar to and different from a real mountain.	4 3 2 1
The student **compared** results and ideas with others.	4 3 2 1
Overall Score	4 3 2 1

Scale Descriptions

4: Student performs the skill with **thorough** understanding.

3: Student performs the skill with **adequate** understanding.

2: Student performs the skill with **basic** understanding.

1: Student performs the skill with **limited** understanding.

Name _____   **Chapter 6**

Inquiry Rubrics — Earth Science

Directed Inquiry
Date _____

Directions: Use the scale descriptions next to the table to guide your assessment of the student's work. Assess each item separately, and then decide on one overall score. Circle the score for each item and the overall score.

Inquiry Rubric	Scale	Scale Descriptions
The student made a **model** of the water cycle and **predicted** what would happen to the model at different stages of the water cycle.	4 3 2 1	**4:** Student performs the skill with **thorough** understanding.
The student **observed** changes in the state of water and recorded both observations and predictions.	4 3 2 1	**3:** Student performs the skill with **adequate** understanding.
The student **compared** predictions with results.	4 3 2 1	**2:** Student performs the skill with **basic** understanding.
The student used the model to draw **conclusions** about how water changes state during the water cycle.	4 3 2 1	**1:** Student performs the skill with **limited** understanding.
The student **shared** and compared observations and conclusions with others.	4 3 2 1	
Overall Score	4 3 2 1	

Guided Inquiry
Date _____

Directions: Use the scale descriptions next to the table to guide your assessment of the student's work. Assess each item separately, and then decide on one overall score. Circle the score for each item and the overall score.

Inquiry Rubric	Scale	Scale Descriptions
The student **measured** a weather condition using the appropriate tool.	4 3 2 1	**4:** Student performs the skill with **thorough** understanding.
The student recorded **data** and **observations** of weather conditions regularly for two weeks.	4 3 2 1	**3:** Student performs the skill with **adequate** understanding.
The student analyzed data to find **patterns** in local weather conditions.	4 3 2 1	**2:** Student performs the skill with **basic** understanding.
The student **predicted** weather based on data and observed patterns.	4 3 2 1	**1:** Student performs the skill with **limited** understanding.
The student **shared** observations and **conclusions** with other students.	4 3 2 1	
Overall Score	4 3 2 1	

Name _____

Inquiry Rubrics Earth Science

Open Inquiry

Date _____

Directions: Use the scale descriptions next to the table to guide your assessment of the student's work. Assess each item separately, and then decide on one overall score. Circle the score for each item and the overall score.

Inquiry Rubric	Scale
The student generated or chose a **question** to **investigate**.	4 3 2 1
The student **planned** an investigation.	4 3 2 1
The student made and **compared observations** and collected and recorded **data**.	4 3 2 1
The student formed a **conclusion** and explained results based on evidence from the collected data and observations.	4 3 2 1
The student **shared** observations and conclusions with other students.	4 3 2 1
Overall Score	4 3 2 1

Scale Descriptions

4: Student performs the skill with **thorough** understanding.

3: Student performs the skill with **adequate** understanding.

2: Student performs the skill with **basic** understanding.

1: Student performs the skill with **limited** understanding.

Name _____ Chapter 1

Explore Activity Self-Reflection — Earth Science

Directions: Write a ✓ in the box to show the answer that is true for you.

	Yes	Not Yet
❶ I can make a model of star movement and use it to make observations.		
❷ I can collect and record data about how stars appear to move.		
❸ I can compare constellations that are visible at different times of night and at the same time of night in different seasons.		
❹ I can compare my observations with those of other students.		
❺ I can share what I observed and concluded with other students.		

Directions: Think about the things you have studied in this chapter. Then finish the sentence.

❻ What did you do well in this investigation? _____

_____

_____

_____

❼ What could your group do differently in the next investigation? _____

_____

_____

_____

Name _____   **Chapter 1**

Directed Inquiry Self-Reflection — Earth Science

Directions: Write a ✓ in the box to show the answer that is true for you.

	Yes	Not Yet
❶ I can make a model of the phases of the moon.		
❷ I can observe the model and record how the model shows the phases of the moon.		
❸ I can find a pattern in the moon phases.		
❹ I can draw a conclusion about the cause of the moon's phases.		
❺ I can share and compare observations and explanations with other students.		

Directions: Think about the things you have studied in this chapter. Then finish the sentence.

❻ What did you like best about this activity? _____

_____

_____

_____

❼ What will you remember to do in your next activity? _____

_____

_____

_____

Name _____   Chapter 2

Directed Inquiry Self-Reflection — Earth Science

Directions: Write a ✓ in the box to show the answer that is true for you.

	Yes	Not Yet
❶ I can observe the color, luster, and streak of each mineral.		
❷ I can use the Mohs scale to observe the hardness of each mineral.		
❸ I can identify each mineral and compare the minerals.		
❹ I can describe the properties that are most useful in identifying the minerals.		
❺ I can share results and conclusions with other students.		

Directions: Think about the things you have studied in this chapter. Then finish the sentence.

❻ What did you like best about observing the minerals? _____

_____

_____

_____

❼ What will you remember most from this activity? _____

_____

_____

_____

Name _____ Chapter 2

Guided Inquiry Self-Reflection — Earth Science

Directions: Write a ✓ in the box to show the answer that is true for you.

	Yes	Not Yet
❶ I can collect and record observations of the rocks.		
❷ I can use physical properties to identify the rocks and classify the rocks as igneous, sedimentary, or metamorphic.		
❸ I can explain how rocks in each group are alike.		
❹ I can compare methods and classifications with other students.		
❺ I can share and compare ideas with other students.		

Directions: Think about the things you have studied in this chapter. Then finish the sentence.

❻ What did you do well? _____

_____

_____

_____

❼ What can you do differently next time you classify rocks? _____

_____

_____

_____

Grade 4 Assessment

Name _____ Chapter 3

Directed Inquiry Self-Reflection — Earth Science

Directions: Write a ✓ in the box to show the answer that is true for you.

	Yes	Not Yet
❶ I can observe three different soil samples and predict which will be best for growing a corn seedling.		
❷ I can measure the growth of seedlings and record observations and data in a table.		
❸ I can compare the prediction with the results.		
❹ I can conclude which soil has the highest fertility based on data and observations.		
❺ I can share and compare what I observed and concluded with other students.		

Directions: Think about the things you have studied in this chapter. Then finish the sentence.

❻ How well did your predictions match your results? _____

_____

_____

_____

❼ Which of your senses was most helpful in observing physical properties of soil? _____

_____

_____

_____

Name _____   Chapter 3

Guided Inquiry Self-Reflection — Earth Science

Directions: Write a ✓ in the box to show the answer that is true for you.

	Yes	Not Yet
❶ I can observe and classify soils.		
❷ I can write a hypothesis about which soil will absorb more water.		
❸ I can measure, collect, and record data about soil absorption.		
❹ I can draw a conclusion about which soil absorbs more water.		
❺ I can share and compare what I observed and concluded with other students.		

Directions: Think about the things you have studied in this chapter. Then finish the sentence.

❻ What about this activity will you think of the next time it rains? _____

_____

_____

_____

❼ How well did your group work together? _____

_____

_____

_____

Name _____   **Chapter 4**

Directed Inquiry Self-Reflection — Earth Science

Directions: Write a ✓ in the box to show the answer that is true for you.

	Yes	Not Yet
❶ I can predict what will happen when sandstone is rubbed together and shaken in water.		
❷ I can observe models of physical weathering, chemical weathering, and erosion.		
❸ I can record observations and compare observations with other students.		
❹ I can use the models to identify examples of physical weathering, chemical weathering, and erosion.		
❺ I can share what I concluded with other students.		

Directions: Think about the things you have studied in this chapter. Then finish the sentence.

❻ What did you do well in this activity? _____

_____

_____

_____

❼ What did you like most about investigating weathering and erosion? _____

_____

_____

_____

Name _____   **Chapter 4**

Guided Inquiry Self-Reflection — Earth Science

Directions: Write a ✓ in the box to show the answer that is true for you.

	Yes	Not Yet
❶ I can make a hypothesis about how water poured on soil affects the movement of soil.		
❷ I can carry out an experiment to test how water poured on soil affects the movement of soil.		
❸ I can make and compare observations and collect and record data about the amount of erosion when water is poured on soil at different rates.		
❹ I can form a conclusion and explain results based on data and observations.		
❺ I can share results with other students.		

Directions: Think about the things you have studied in this chapter. Then finish the sentence.

❻ How did your results support your hypothesis? _____

_____

_____

_____

❼ How would you improve this experiment? _____

_____

_____

_____

Name _____

Chapter 5

Directed Inquiry Self-Reflection — Earth Science

Directions: Write a ✓ in the box to show the answer that is true for you.

	Yes	Not Yet
❶ I can make and use a model to learn more about earthquakes.		
❷ I can make predictions about the motion of the blocks.		
❸ I can understand and follow safety procedures.		
❹ I can share methods, data, and results with other students.		
❺ I can draw conclusions about earthquakes based on the model.		

Directions: Think about the things you have studied in this chapter. Then finish the sentence.

❻ What did you do well in this investigation? _____

_____

_____

_____

❼ What could your group do differently in the next investigation? _____

_____

_____

_____

Name _____   **Chapter 5**

Guided Inquiry Self-Reflection — Earth Science

Directions: Write a ✓ in the box to show the answer that is true for you.

	Yes	Not Yet
❶ I can use a model to investigate how some types of mountains form.		
❷ I can predict how different amounts of force will change the model.		
❸ I can draw conclusions about how mountains form.		
❹ I can explain how the model is similar to and different from a real mountain.		
❺ I can compare results and ideas with other students.		

Directions: Think about the things you have studied in this chapter. Then finish the sentence.

❻ What about this activity will you think of the next time you see a mountain? _____

_____

_____

_____

❼ How would you improve this activity? _____

_____

_____

_____

_____

Grade 4 Assessment

Name _____

Chapter 6

Directed Inquiry Self-Reflection — Earth Science

Directions: Write a ✓ in the box to show the answer that is true for you.

	Yes	Not Yet
❶ I can make a model of the water cycle and predict what will happen to the model at different steps of the water cycle.		
❷ I can observe changes in the state of water and record what I observed and predicted.		
❸ I can compare predictions with results.		
❹ I can use the model to draw conclusions about how water changes state during the water cycle.		
❺ I can share and compare what I observed and concluded with other students.		

Directions: Think about the things you have studied in this chapter. Then finish the sentence.

❻ What surprised you about how water changes? _____

_____

_____

_____

❼ How can you tell the difference between an observation, prediction, and inference? _____

_____

_____

_____

Grade 4 Assessment

Name _____ Chapter 6

Guided Inquiry Self-Reflection — Earth Science

Directions: Write a ✓ in the box to show the answer that is true for you.

	Yes	Not Yet
❶ I can measure a weather condition using the appropriate tool.		
❷ I can record data and observations of weather conditions regularly for two weeks.		
❸ I can analyze data to find patterns in local weather conditions.		
❹ I can predict weather based on data and observed patterns.		
❺ I can share what I observed and concluded with other students.		

Directions: Think about the things you have studied in this chapter. Then finish the sentence.

❻ Which tools did you find most helpful? _____

_____

_____

_____

❼ What about this activity will you think of the next time it rains? _____

_____

_____

_____

Grade 4 Assessment

Name _____

Open Inquiry Self-Reflection — Earth Science

Directions: Write a ✓ in the box to show the answer that is true for you.

	Yes	Not Yet
❶ I can think of or choose a question to investigate.		
❷ I can plan an investigation by identifying, changing, and controlling variables.		
❸ I can make and compare observations and collect and record data.		
❹ I can form a conclusion and explain results based on data and observations.		
❺ I can share observations and conclusions with other students.		

Directions: Think about the things you have studied in this unit. Then finish the sentence.

❻ What do you like best about your investigation? _____

_____

_____

_____

❼ What will you remember most from this activity? _____

_____

_____

_____

Name _____ Chapter 1

Inquiry Rubrics Physical Science

Explore Activity
Date _____

Directions: Use the scale descriptions next to the table to guide your assessment of the student's work. Assess each item separately, and then decide on one overall score. Circle the score for each item and the overall score.

Inquiry Rubric	Scale
The student **observed** the mixture and the materials that made it up.	4 3 2 1
The student separated the parts of the mixture using the properties of the different materials and recorded their observations.	4 3 2 1
The student worked with a group to solve the problem, giving credit to the ideas and contributions of each group member.	4 3 2 1
The student made an **inference** about salt remaining in the cup after the water evaporated.	4 3 2 1
The student **shared** observations and inferences with others.	4 3 2 1
Overall Score	4 3 2 1

Scale Descriptions

4: Student performs the skill with **thorough** understanding.

3: Student performs the skill with **adequate** understanding.

2: Student performs the skill with **basic** understanding.

1: Student performs the skill with **limited** understanding.

Directed Inquiry
Date _____

Directions: Use the scale descriptions next to the table to guide your assessment of the student's work. Assess each item separately, and then decide on one overall score. Circle the score for each item and the overall score.

Inquiry Rubric	Scale
The student **measured** and recorded **data** about the volume of ice and water.	4 3 2 1
The student measured and recorded data about the mass of ice and water.	4 3 2 1
The student **compared** observations of the volume and mass of ice and water.	4 3 2 1
The student formed a **conclusion** about how changing the state of water affects its volume and mass.	4 3 2 1
The student **shared** observations and conclusions with others.	4 3 2 1
Overall Score	4 3 2 1

Scale Descriptions

4: Student performs the skill with **thorough** understanding.

3: Student performs the skill with **adequate** understanding.

2: Student performs the skill with **basic** understanding.

1: Student performs the skill with **limited** understanding.

Name _____ **Chapter 2**

Inquiry Rubrics Physical Science

Directed Inquiry

Date _____

Directions: Use the scale descriptions next to the table to guide your assessment of the student's work. Assess each item separately, and then decide on one overall score. Circle the score for each item and the overall score.

Inquiry Rubric	Scale			
The student **observed** properties of solid ice, liquid water, and water vapor.	4	3	2	1
The student **predicted** how the properties of water would change as it sat in the sunlight.	4	3	2	1
The student **inferred** what caused the water to change its state.	4	3	2	1
The student clearly distinguished between observations, predictions, and inferences.	4	3	2	1
The student **shared** observations and **conclusions** with other students.	4	3	2	1
Overall Score	4	3	2	1

Scale Descriptions

4: Student performs the skill with **thorough** understanding.

3: Student performs the skill with **adequate** understanding.

2: Student performs the skill with **basic** understanding.

1: Student performs the skill with **limited** understanding.

Guided Inquiry

Date _____

Directions: Use the scale descriptions next to the table to guide your assessment of the student's work. Assess each item separately, and then decide on one overall score. Circle the score for each item and the overall score.

Inquiry Rubric	Scale			
The student carried out an **experiment** to determine what happens when steel wool rusts.	4	3	2	1
The student recorded **observations** of the water levels in the test tubes.	4	3	2	1
The student made an **inference** about the causes of rusting.	4	3	2	1
The student used observations and **data** to support inferences and **conclusions**.	4	3	2	1
The student **shared** results and **compared** observations and data with other students.	4	3	2	1
Overall Score	4	3	2	1

Scale Descriptions

4: Student performs the skill with **thorough** understanding.

3: Student performs the skill with **adequate** understanding.

2: Student performs the skill with **basic** understanding.

1: Student performs the skill with **limited** understanding.

Name _____   Chapter 3

Inquiry Rubrics — Physical Science

Directed Inquiry   Date _____

Directions: Use the scale descriptions next to the table to guide your assessment of the student's work. Assess each item separately, and then decide on one overall score. Circle the score for each item and the overall score.

Inquiry Rubric	Scale	Scale Descriptions
The student **observed** how the motion of the car changed in response to magnetic forces.	4 3 2 1	**4:** Student performs the skill with **thorough** understanding.
The student observed how the motion changed when an equal and opposite force was applied to the car.	4 3 2 1	**3:** Student performs the skill with **adequate** understanding.
The student **compared data** from multiple trials and offered explanations for any variations.	4 3 2 1	**2:** Student performs the skill with **basic** understanding.
The student **concluded** that the magnet exerted force that acted over a distance and the index card applied an equal and opposite force to the car.	4 3 2 1	**1:** Student performs the skill with **limited** understanding.
The student **shared** results and used quantitative and qualitative data to support conclusions.	4 3 2 1	
Overall Score	4 3 2 1	

Guided Inquiry   Date _____

Directions: Use the scale descriptions next to the table to guide your assessment of the student's work. Assess each item separately, and then decide on one overall score. Circle the score for each item and the overall score.

Inquiry Rubric	Scale	Scale Descriptions
The student made a **hypothesis** about how different materials would affect the motion of the toy car.	4 3 2 1	**4:** Student performs the skill with **thorough** understanding.
The student identified which **variable** to change, which variable to measure, and which variable to keep the same.	4 3 2 1	**3:** Student performs the skill with **adequate** understanding.
The student selected the best tool to **measure** the car's change in position.	4 3 2 1	**2:** Student performs the skill with **basic** understanding.
The student **compared data** among groups to analyze the car's change in motion and position on three different materials.	4 3 2 1	**1:** Student performs the skill with **limited** understanding.
The student **shared conclusions** about how different surfaces affected the motion of the car.	4 3 2 1	
Overall Score	4 3 2 1	

Grade 4 Assessment

Name _____   Chapter 4

Inquiry Rubrics Physical Science

Directed Inquiry   Date _____

Directions: Use the scale descriptions next to the table to guide your assessment of the student's work. Assess each item separately, and then decide on one overall score. Circle the score for each item and the overall score.

Inquiry Rubric	Scale			
The student demonstrated that opposite poles of a magnet attract each other and the same poles repel each other.	4	3	2	1
The student demonstrated that a magnet attracts paper clips.	4	3	2	1
The student recorded **predictions** and **observations** in a table and **compared** the **data**.	4	3	2	1
The student wrote an **operational definition** for a magnet.	4	3	2	1
The student **shared** results and **conclusions** with other students.	4	3	2	1
Overall Score	4	3	2	1

Scale Descriptions

4: Student performs the skill with **thorough** understanding.

3: Student performs the skill with **adequate** understanding.

2: Student performs the skill with **basic** understanding.

1: Student performs the skill with **limited** understanding.

Guided Inquiry   Date _____

Directions: Use the scale descriptions next to the table to guide your assessment of the student's work. Assess each item separately, and then decide on one overall score. Circle the score for each item and the overall score.

Inquiry Rubric	Scale			
The student **observed** how iron filings line up in reaction to different magnets and their magnetic fields.	4	3	2	1
The student observed how iron filings line up between like and opposite poles.	4	3	2	1
The student made **predictions** and compared them with results.	4	3	2	1
The student **compared** drawings and observations with other students.	4	3	2	1
The student drew **conclusions** about how the different magnets and poles attracted or repelled each other.	4	3	2	1
Overall Score	4	3	2	1

Scale Descriptions

4: Student performs the skill with **thorough** understanding.

3: Student performs the skill with **adequate** understanding.

2: Student performs the skill with **basic** understanding.

1: Student performs the skill with **limited** understanding.

Name _____   Chapter 5

Inquiry Rubrics — Physical Science

Directed Inquiry
Date _____

Directions: Use the scale descriptions next to the table to guide your assessment of the student's work. Assess each item separately, and then decide on one overall score. Circle the score for each item and the overall score.

Inquiry Rubric	Scale
The student **observed** the different forms of energy.	4 3 2 1
The student identified and described different forms of energy.	4 3 2 1
The student **inferred** what caused the spiral to move.	4 3 2 1
The student inferred that energy has the ability to cause motion or create change.	4 3 2 1
The student **shared** results, inferences, and ideas with others.	4 3 2 1
Overall Score	4 3 2 1

Scale Descriptions

4: Student performs the skill with **thorough** understanding.

3: Student performs the skill with **adequate** understanding.

2: Student performs the skill with **basic** understanding.

1: Student performs the skill with **limited** understanding.

Guided Inquiry
Date _____

Directions: Use the scale descriptions next to the table to guide your assessment of the student's work. Assess each item separately, and then decide on one overall score. Circle the score for each item and the overall score.

Inquiry Rubric	Scale
The student **observed** the color changes in the strip thermometers.	4 3 2 1
The student **compared** how plastic, metal, and wood rulers conduct heat.	4 3 2 1
The student compared how the strip thermometers changed when exposed to different temperatures of water.	4 3 2 1
The student **inferred** what caused the changes in the color of the strip thermometer.	4 3 2 1
The student **shared** results and compared ideas with others and explained any differences.	4 3 2 1
Overall Score	4 3 2 1

Scale Descriptions

4: Student performs the skill with **thorough** understanding.

3: Student performs the skill with **adequate** understanding.

2: Student performs the skill with **basic** understanding.

1: Student performs the skill with **limited** understanding.

Name _____   **Chapter 6**

Inquiry Rubrics — Physical Science

Directed Inquiry

Date _____

Directions: Use the scale descriptions next to the table to guide your assessment of the student's work. Assess each item separately, and then decide on one overall score. Circle the score for each item and the overall score.

Inquiry Rubric	Scale			
The student **predicted** how the pitch and vibration of a fishing line would change.	4	3	2	1
The student **observed** the pitch that was created when a fishing line was plucked.	4	3	2	1
The student recorded **data** in a table.	4	3	2	1
The student made an **inference** about why the tightness of the fishing line changed the sound.	4	3	2	1
The student **shared** and **compared** predictions and inferences with others.	4	3	2	1
Overall Score	4	3	2	1

Scale Descriptions

4: Student performs the skill with **thorough** understanding.

3: Student performs the skill with **adequate** understanding.

2: Student performs the skill with **basic** understanding.

1: Student performs the skill with **limited** understanding.

Guided Inquiry

Date _____

Directions: Use the scale descriptions next to the table to guide your assessment of the student's work. Assess each item separately, and then decide on one overall score. Circle the score for each item and the overall score.

Inquiry Rubric	Scale			
The student used a straw to make a musical instrument.	4	3	2	1
The student **inferred** that the vibrations caused sounds in the straw instrument.	4	3	2	1
The student made a **plan** to change the instrument design in order to change its pitch.	4	3	2	1
The student carried out the plan and recorded **observations** about pitch.	4	3	2	1
The student **shared** and **compared** observations, inferences, and results with other students.	4	3	2	1
Overall Score	4	3	2	1

Scale Descriptions

4: Student performs the skill with **thorough** understanding.

3: Student performs the skill with **adequate** understanding.

2: Student performs the skill with **basic** understanding.

1: Student performs the skill with **limited** understanding.

Name _____   Chapter 7

Inquiry Rubrics | Physical Science

Directed Inquiry   Date _____

Directions: Use the scale descriptions next to the table to guide your assessment of the student's work. Assess each item separately, and then decide on one overall score. Circle the score for each item and the overall score.

Inquiry Rubric	Scale				Scale Descriptions
The student **predicted** what would happen when one light bulb was unscrewed in a parallel and series circuit.	4	3	2	1	4: Student performs the skill with **thorough** understanding.
The student **observed** and diagrammed a parallel and series circuit.	4	3	2	1	3: Student performs the skill with **adequate** understanding.
The student **shared** and **compared** predictions and observations.	4	3	2	1	2: Student performs the skill with **basic** understanding.
The student compared parallel circuits with series circuits.	4	3	2	1	1: Student performs the skill with **limited** understanding.
The student drew a **conclusion** about why parallel circuits are more commonly used than series circuits.	4	3	2	1	
Overall Score	4	3	2	1	

Guided Inquiry   Date _____

Directions: Use the scale descriptions next to the table to guide your assessment of the student's work. Assess each item separately, and then decide on one overall score. Circle the score for each item and the overall score.

Inquiry Rubric	Scale				Scale Descriptions
The student **observed** an open and a closed circuit.	4	3	2	1	4: Student performs the skill with **thorough** understanding.
The student **classified** three materials as conductors or insulators.	4	3	2	1	3: Student performs the skill with **adequate** understanding.
The student created an **operational definition** of a conductor and an insulator.	4	3	2	1	2: Student performs the skill with **basic** understanding.
The student **compared** observations about which materials completed the circuit and which did not.	4	3	2	1	1: Student performs the skill with **limited** understanding.
The student **shared data** and **conclusions** with others.	4	3	2	1	
Overall Score	4	3	2	1	

Name _____

Inquiry Rubrics — Physical Science

Open Inquiry

Date _____

Directions: Use the scale descriptions next to the table to guide your assessment of the student's work. Assess each item separately, and then decide on one overall score. Circle the score for each item and the overall score.

Inquiry Rubric	Scale			
The student generated or chose a **question** to **investigate**.	4	3	2	1
The student **planned** and carried out an **experiment** by identifying, manipulating, and controlling **variables**.	4	3	2	1
The student made and **compared observations** and collected and recorded **data**.	4	3	2	1
The student formed a **conclusion** and explained results based on evidence from the collected data and observations.	4	3	2	1
The student **shared** observations and conclusions with other students.	4	3	2	1
Overall Score	4	3	2	1

Scale Descriptions

4: Student performs the skill with **thorough** understanding.

3: Student performs the skill with **adequate** understanding.

2: Student performs the skill with **basic** understanding.

1: Student performs the skill with **limited** understanding.

Name _____

Chapter 1

Explore Activity Self-Reflection — Physical Science

Directions: Write a ✓ in the box to show the answer that is true for you.

	Yes	Not Yet
❶ I can observe a mixture and the materials that make it up.		
❷ I can separate the parts of a mixture using the properties of the different materials and record my observations.		
❸ I can work with a group to solve a problem and say how each group member helped.		
❹ I can make an inference about salt remaining in a cup after the water evaporated.		
❺ I can share observations and inferences with other students.		

Directions: Think about the things you have studied in this chapter. Then finish the sentence.

❻ What did you like best about this investigation? _____

_____

_____

_____

❼ How well did your group work together? _____

_____

_____

_____

Name _____

Chapter 1

Directed Inquiry Self-Reflection — Physical Science

Directions: Write a ✓ in the box to show the answer that is true for you.

	Yes	Not Yet
❶ I can measure and record data about the volume of ice and water.		
❷ I can measure and record data about the mass of ice and water.		
❸ I can compare observations of the volume and mass of ice and water.		
❹ I can make a conclusion about how changing the state of water affects its volume and mass.		
❺ I can share what I observed and concluded with other students.		

Directions: Think about the things you have studied in this chapter. Then finish the sentence.

❻ What will you remember about measuring for your next activity? _____

_____

_____

_____

❼ What surprised you about how water changes? _____

_____

_____

_____

Grade 4 Assessment

Name _____   **Chapter 2**

Directed Inquiry Self-Reflection Physical Science

Directions: Write a ✓ in the box to show the answer that is true for you.

	Yes	Not Yet
❶ I can observe properties of solid ice, liquid water, and water vapor.		
❷ I can predict how the properties of water will change as it sits in the sunlight.		
❸ I can infer what causes water to change its state.		
❹ I can tell the difference between observations, predictions, and inferences.		
❺ I can share observations and conclusions with other students.		

Directions: Think about the things you have studied in this chapter. Then finish the sentence.

❻ What did you do well? _____

_____

_____

_____

❼ How would you improve this activity? _____

_____

_____

_____

Grade 4 Assessment

Name _____

Chapter 2

Guided Inquiry Self-Reflection — Physical Science

Directions: Write a ✓ in the box to show the answer that is true for you.

	Yes	Not Yet
❶ I can do an experiment to find out what happens when steel wool rusts.		
❷ I can record observations of the water levels in the test tubes.		
❸ I can make an inference about the causes of rusting.		
❹ I can use observations and data to support inferences and conclusions.		
❺ I can share results and compare observations and data with other students.		

Directions: Think about the things you have studied in this chapter. Then finish the sentence.

❻ How well did your group work together? _____

_____

_____

_____

❼ What did you like best about your experiment? _____

_____

_____

_____

Grade 4 Assessment

Name _____   **Chapter 3**

Directed Inquiry Self-Reflection — Physical Science

Directions: Write a ✓ in the box to show the answer that is true for you.

	Yes	Not Yet
❶ I can observe how the motion of a toy car is affected by different poles of a magnet at different distances.		
❷ I can observe how the motion changes when a toy car hits another object.		
❸ I can compare data from several trials and explain any differences.		
❹ I can conclude that a magnet can move objects without touching them and that other objects can stop the movement.		
❺ I can share results and use data to support conclusions.		

Directions: Think about the things you have studied in this chapter. Then finish the sentence.

❻ What did you learn in this activity that will help you keep records in the future? _____

_____

_____

_____

❼ What did you do well? _____

_____

_____

_____

Name _____   **Chapter 3**

Guided Inquiry Self-Reflection — Physical Science

Directions: Write a ✓ in the box to show the answer that is true for you.

	Yes	Not Yet
❶ I can make a hypothesis about how different materials will affect the motion of a toy car.		
❷ I can identify which variable to change, which variable to measure, and which variable to keep the same.		
❸ I can choose the best tool to measure the car's change in position.		
❹ I can compare data from other groups to figure out how different materials affect a toy car's motion and position.		
❺ I can share what I concluded about how different surfaces affected the motion of the car.		

Directions: Think about the things you have studied in this chapter. Then finish the sentence.

❻ How would you improve this activity? _____

_____

_____

_____

❼ How well did your group work together? _____

_____

_____

_____

Name _____   **Chapter 4**

Directed Inquiry Self-Reflection — Physical Science

Directions: Write a ✓ in the box to show the answer that is true for you.

	Yes	Not Yet
❶ I can demonstrate that opposite poles of a magnet attract each other and the same poles repel each other.		
❷ I can demonstrate that a magnet attracts paper clips.		
❸ I can record predictions and observations in a table and compare the data.		
❹ I can write an operational definition for a magnet.		
❺ I can share results and conclusions with other students.		

Directions: Think about the things you have studied in this chapter. Then finish the sentence.

❻ What could you do to help your group work together better? _____

_____

_____

_____

❼ What do you like best about your data table? _____

_____

_____

_____

Grade 4 Assessment

Name _____   **Chapter 4**

Guided Inquiry Self-Reflection — Physical Science

Directions: Write a ✓ in the box to show the answer that is true for you.

	Yes	Not Yet
❶ I can observe how iron filings line up when placed near different magnets and their magnetic fields.		
❷ I can observe how iron filings line up between the same poles and opposite poles.		
❸ I can make predictions and compare them with results.		
❹ I can compare drawings and observations with other students.		
❺ I can draw conclusions about how the different magnets and poles attracted or repelled each other.		

Directions: Think about the things you have studied in this chapter. Then finish the sentence.

❻ How could you tell the difference between an observation, prediction, and inference? _____

_____

_____

_____

❼ What could you do to help your group work together better? _____

_____

_____

_____

Name _____ Chapter 5

Directed Inquiry Self-Reflection — Physical Science

Directions: Write a ✓ in the box to show the answer that is true for you.

	Yes	Not Yet
❶ I can observe the different forms of energy.		
❷ I can identify and describe different forms of energy.		
❸ I can infer what causes a foil spiral held above a lamp to move.		
❹ I can infer that energy has the ability to cause motion or create change.		
❺ I can share results, inferences, and ideas with others.		

Directions: Think about the things you have studied in this chapter. Then finish the sentence.

❻ How would you improve this activity? _____

_____

_____

_____

❼ What will you remember most from this activity? _____

_____

_____

_____

Name _____   **Chapter 5**

Guided Inquiry Self-Reflection — Physical Science

Directions: Write a ✓ in the box to show the answer that is true for you.

	Yes	Not Yet
❶ I can observe color changes in strip thermometers.		
❷ I can compare how plastic, metal, and wood rulers conduct heat.		
❸ I can compare how strip thermometers change when put in water of different temperatures.		
❹ I can infer what causes changes in the color of a strip thermometer.		
❺ I can share results and compare ideas with others and explain any differences.		

Directions: Think about the things you have studied in this chapter. Then finish the sentence.

❻ How well did your group work together? _____

_____

_____

_____

❼ What will you remember to do in your next activity? _____

_____

_____

_____

Grade 4 Assessment

Name _____ **Chapter 6**

Directed Inquiry Self-Reflection — Physical Science

Directions: Write a ✓ in the box to show the answer that is true for you.

	Yes	Not Yet
❶ I can predict how the pitch and vibration of a fishing line will change.		
❷ I can observe the pitch that is created when a fishing line is plucked.		
❸ I can record data in a table.		
❹ I can make an inference about why the tightness of the fishing line changes the sound.		
❺ I can share and compare predictions and inferences with others.		

Directions: Think about the things you have studied in this chapter. Then finish the sentence.

❻ What do you like best about your table? _____
_____
_____
_____

❼ What will you remember to do in your next activity? _____
_____
_____
_____

Name _____   **Chapter 6**

Guided Inquiry Self-Reflection — Physical Science

Directions: Write a ✓ in the box to show the answer that is true for you.

	Yes	Not Yet
❶ I can use a straw to make a musical instrument.		
❷ I can infer that vibrations cause sounds in the straw instrument.		
❸ I can make a plan to change an instrument's design in order to change its pitch.		
❹ I can carry out a plan and record observations about pitch.		
❺ I can share and compare observations, inferences, and results with other students.		

Directions: Think about the things you have studied in this chapter. Then finish the sentence.

❻ What could you do to help your group work together better? _____

_____

_____

_____

❼ What did you do well? _____

_____

_____

_____

241   Grade 4 Assessment

Name _____   **Chapter 7**

Directed Inquiry Self-Reflection — Physical Science

Directions: Write a ✓ in the box to show the answer that is true for you.

	Yes	Not Yet
1 I can predict what will happen when one light bulb is unscrewed in a parallel and series circuit.		
2 I can observe and draw a diagram of a parallel and series circuit.		
3 I can share and compare predictions and observations.		
4 I can compare parallel circuits with series circuits.		
5 I can draw a conclusion about why parallel circuits are more commonly used than series circuits.		

Directions: Think about the things you have studied in this chapter. Then finish the sentence.

6 What will you remember most from this activity? _____

_____

_____

_____

7 How could you record your observations more accurately? _____

_____

_____

_____

Name _____   **Chapter 7**

Guided Inquiry Self-Reflection   Physical Science

Directions: Write a ✓ in the box to show the answer that is true for you.

	Yes	Not Yet
❶ I can observe an open and a closed circuit.		
❷ I can classify three materials as conductors or insulators.		
❸ I can create an operational definition for a conductor and an insulator.		
❹ I can compare observations about which materials can complete a circuit and which cannot.		
❺ I can share data and conclusions with other students.		

Directions: Think about the things you have studied in this chapter. Then finish the sentence.

❻ How would you improve this activity? _____

_____

_____

_____

❼ What was the most interesting thing you learned from sharing your conclusions with other students?

_____

_____

_____

Name _____

Open Inquiry Self-Reflection — Physical Science

Directions: Write a ✓ in the box to show the answer that is true for you.

	Yes	Not Yet
❶ I can think of or choose a question to investigate.		
❷ I can plan an investigation by identifying, changing, and controlling variables.		
❸ I can make and compare observations and collect and record data.		
❹ I can form a conclusion and explain results based on data and observations.		
❺ I can share observations and conclusions with other students.		

Directions: Think about the things you have studied in this unit. Then finish the sentence.

❻ What do you like best about your investigation? _____

_____

_____

_____

❼ What will you remember most from this activity? _____

_____

_____

_____